"With the help of pulleys and improvised shears [hoisting devices] we were with difficulty able to raise the fallen portion so as to enable me to mold the glyphs on the underside." [Copán]

"On the first, second, and top floors there are wide openings or doorways through each of the four walls. These were formerly capped by wooden lintels." [Palenque]

"On our arrival at the ruins [of Palenque] we found both the East and West Courts filled up...with broken masonry that had fallen from the surrounding buildings."

"This house [House A, Palenque] stands on the northern half of the east side of the Palace Mound. It consists of two parallel corridors divided by a main wall."

"The ornament of the frieze [Temple of the Sun, Palenque]... is very much damaged; but it is possible to make out part of the body and the head of a great serpent."

"There is considerable difficulty in obtaining accurate measurements of the Castillo [in Chichén Itzá], owing to the large amount of fallen stone."

"In spite of the hard work, the worry about laborers, and the attack of fever, I cannot help looking back on my stay at Chichén with considerable pleasure and satisfaction."

CONTENTS

LOST CITIES OF
THE MAYA

Claude Baudez and Sydney Picasso

DISCOVERIES

HARRY N. ABRAMS, INC., PUBLISHERS

NEW YORK

I t was 1502—or the second year of *katun 2 ahau*, according to the Maya calendar. Twenty-five Indians, packed into an open canoe carved from a giant tree trunk, were making their way east towards the island of Guanaja. There, in the Gulf of Honduras, a strange meeting was about to take place.

CHAPTER I

CONQUISTADORS AND MISSIONARIES

T his late-18th-century painting presents things from the conquerors' point of view: the Spanish dominate the composition, while the Indians, who look more like children, are relegated to the shadows. In the center, the imposing figure of Juan de Grijalva condescends to bless the frail and submissive cacique of Tabasco, an archetypal "noble savage," who is shown barefoot and wearing a short skirt and a plumed headdress.

On board the boat, the Indian chief was sitting in the shade of a canopy surrounded by his retinue of men, women, and children. He was en route from the Yucatán to trade with the natives of the coast and islands. Slaves, roped together at the neck, paddled along in unison. Bundles of goods to be bartered were piled in the bottom of the boat: brightly colored cotton clothing, flint knives, hardwood swords with their edges inlaid with sharp blades. At the chief's feet lay cacao beans, small axes, and little copper bells—the most precious items in the cargo.

Suddenly one of the men cried out in surprise. In all the time he had been sailing these waters he had never noticed the three great reefs off Guanaja. A moment later one of his companions gave an even louder cry; he thought he had seen one of the reefs move. Suddenly, the paddlers stopped stock still and exchanged worried glances. The chief silently gave the signal to continue. On the islands, which looked like large, half-submerged bowls, stood tall, bare tree trunks from which hung a network of ropes. The islands were obviously inhabited; human forms could be seen moving above the dark masses. Were they people or gods? All that could be seen of the creatures were their faces and hands, and their faces—the Indians soon discovered—were often covered with hair, like a monkey's.

Bravely, the expedition approached the floating mountains. At their summit the creatures began to point and talk in loud voices. Could these reefs be vast boats that the creatures had built themselves? Rope ladders were thrown down, and the Indians were invited to go aboard. The chief set an example by clambering up. Gifts were exchanged. There was amazement on both sides; they stared at each other, felt each other's clothes, skin, and ornaments. The

Columbus (1451–1506) devoted his life to the search for new lands. He dreamed of reaching China (Cathay) and Japan (Cipangu).

strangers could not speak the Indians' language, so they pointed in the direction from which the canoe had come, and the Indians replied *maiam.*

This was the first contact between the Maya of the Yucatán peninsula and the sailing ships of Christopher Columbus, anchored off Guanaja. The great explorer of the West Indies was on his fourth voyage of discovery.

Nine Years After This Brief Encounter the First Spaniards Landed on Maya Soil

The first Europeans to set foot in "Mayathan" were not conquerors, but the survivors of a shipwreck off the coast of Jamaica. They landed in a pitiful state on a Yucatán beach opposite the island of Cozumel, after drifting in an open boat for thirteen days, having watched half of their companions die from thirst and hunger.

They had scarcely come ashore when they were greeted by a band of Indians, who thanked the gods for sending them these sacrificial victims so

"We climbed up a tree to get a better look, and we must tell you that we saw a house in the water, out of which came white men, with white hands and faces, and very long, bushy beards, and clothes of every color: white, yellow, and red, green, blue, and purple;…and on their heads they wore round hats."

Report by two Aztec spies to their king Moctezuma

opportunely. Admittedly, they were not in very good condition, as victims went, but they were of such an unusual type…and this would surely appeal to the gods. Half of the shipwrecked sailors perished on the altar, their chests slit open and their hearts torn out, while the remainder were imprisoned in a cage. As they waited for the next festival, when they, too, would be sacrificed, the prisoners were given all the food they could eat to help them regain the weight they had lost during the previous weeks. Two of them survived. Gerónimo de Aguilar became the slave of a chief, who spared his life in return for his devoted service, and Gonzalo Guerrero became the war leader of another town, married, and had a family, becoming completely integrated into Maya culture.

The Spanish Were Lucky to Have Begun on the Islands—the More Organized Peoples on the Mainland Would Have Crushed Them

Having soon massacred or reduced to slavery the populations of Cuba and Hispaniola (today divided between Haiti and the Dominican Republic), the Europeans used these islands as a secure base from which to launch expeditions. Hernández de Córdoba's voyage of 1517 was one such raid. Córdoba went in search of slaves, which were already in short supply on the islands, and also—with luck—of gold. He sailed west and landed on an island which, like Cozumel, lay not far from the northeast coast of the Yucatán peninsula. The Spaniards were amazed to find evidence of civilization on the island in the form of

Hernández de Córdoba, in search of slaves and gold.

"When Francisco Hernández de Córdoba reached this country, he met some Indian fishermen and asked them the name of the place; they replied *cotoch,* which means "our homes, our land." That is where the name of this headland came from. When Córdoba indicated by hand signs that he wished to know more about the country, they replied *ci uthan,* meaning "so they say." The Spanish named it Yucatán."

Diego de Landa,
Relación de las Cosas de Yucatán, 1566

permanent
structures,
which were in
marked contrast to the simple
huts of the Caribbean. They named the place Isla
Mujeres, the Isle of Women, because the temples they
visited there contained numerous female idols. The
few gold objects they managed to find were later used
to justify further raids on the region.

Córdoba then sailed north, rounding the peninsula
and following the coast to the town of Champotón at
its base. Once on land, the Spaniards were fiercely
attacked by the Maya. Córdoba replied with the ship's
artillery, but when they had recovered from this
baptism of fire, the Maya rallied and inflicted heavy

The Spanish were
horrified by the
spectacle of human
sacrifice practiced by the
peoples of Mesoamerica.
They saw it as positive
proof that the land was in
the Devil's clutches. At
the time of the Conquest
and for five centuries
before it, the most
common form taken by
this ritual was extraction
of the heart.

losses on their adversaries. Córdoba died soon afterwards, in Cuba, from the thirty-three wounds he had received in the battle.

Following the return of this expedition, the inhabitants of Cuba could think of nothing but the piles of gold on Isla Mujeres. The Spanish later discovered that Yucatán soil concealed not the slightest trace of gold; the treasures carried off by Córdoba must have come from Honduras or the regions much further south that traded with the Maya. For the time being, however, the governor of Cuba, Diego Velásquez, took the rumors seriously. He armed four ships and recruited two hundred men under the command of his nephew, Juan de Grijalva.

This time when the fleet reached Cozumel it followed the coast south; believing the Yucatán to be an island, Grijalva initially tried to sail around it. The expedition got as far as Ascension Bay (Quintana Roo) before retracing the route and sailing right around the peninsula again to Champotón.

There was another battle, resulting in severe defeat for the Spanish, who set sail once more until they reached the Río Panuco, some 600 miles to the northwest. Grijalva was determined that there should be no pillaging, that they should fight only when forced to,

Convinced of his divine mission, Hernán Cortés (left) was quite different from the plunderers who had explored the New World before him. He combined the authority and persuasive powers of a great leader, the bravery and cunning of an experienced soldier, and the judgment and skill of a diplomat.

At the beginning of the 16th century the Aztecs were the major power in Mesoamerica. Yet their origins were modest; they began as a tribe of seminomadic hunters.

It was Diego Velásquez, the elderly and acquisitive governor of Cuba, who made his former secretary Cortés' fortune, by putting him in charge of the third expedition to Mexico. He chose Cortés because of his enterprising and determined character, but also because he had complete confidence in him. Soon, however, Velásquez heard rumors of Cortés' desire for independence and determined to strip him of his command. When he heard this, Cortés hurriedly loaded up his fleet and weighed anchor that very day. For three months he sailed around the island, in defiance of Velásquez' orders, taking on the men he still needed and collecting provisions. Then he set sail for the Yucatán.

and above all that they should trade with the Indians.

There followed episodic contact with the native inhabitants of various countries, who were sometimes welcoming, sometimes hostile. And it was in the course of this five-month voyage that the Europeans first learned of the wealth and power of the Aztecs.

Determined to Conquer the Maya, The Spanish Invested in Ever-Larger Expeditions

On 18 February 1519 Hernán Cortés set sail with 11 ships, 508 men, and 16 horses. In Cozumel he learned that bearded men were living only six days' journey away. He sent a message to them, but having had no reply, he decided to get under way once more. However, he was soon forced to return to port to repair a leaking hull, and while he was there Gerónimo de Aguilar arrived, weeping for joy and thanking God. His most immediate concern was to find out whether or not it was a Wednesday; for eight years he had kept a record of the days of the Christian calendar. Gonzalo Guerrero, on the other hand, refused to leave his new family and adopted people.

With the same pilot as for the two previous expeditions, the ships sailed north, rounding the peninsula, and, leaving Maya territory behind them, followed the coasts of Tabasco and Veracruz. Cortés soon landed—for good—on Mexican soil, setting fire to his ships to discourage any hesitant soldiers from deserting, and set out to conquer the Aztec empire, which would be brought to its knees within a year. By contrast, it took the Spanish twenty years to conquer the Yucatán. Relatively few in number, they went from group to group, demanding that the natives swear allegiance to the Spanish crown. Though they were often received with volleys of arrows, they were able to exploit the hatred that existed between rival tribes in this divided country.

The Missionaries Studied the Customs of the Maya, Believing That to Destroy the Work of the Devil, One Must First Understand It

In 1546 Tutul Xiu, the most powerful chief in the province of Maní, the main political unit of north Yucatán, submitted to the Spanish and was converted to Christianity. The princes of the western half of the peninsula followed his example. All that now remained was to pacify the rebellious eastern provinces, and this would not be easy. It took several months and many battles.

The main justification for the conquest of the Yucatán, as for the whole New World, was to spread Christianity. The men of God often rose up to protest against the methods employed by those who wielded the sword. There were many priests who, like Bartolomeo de las Casas (below), protested against the harsh treatment the Indians received from the Spanish.

Of all the Spaniards involved in the conquest and colonization of the country, it was the churchmen who showed the most interest in the Maya and their civilization. The first Franciscans had landed there in 1535. In order to lead the natives to the true faith, they had to eliminate anything that might distract them from the path to God. Idols were destroyed, temples burned, and those who celebrated the native rites and practiced sacrifice were punished by death; festivities, such as banquets, songs, and dances, as well as artistic and intellectual activities (painting, sculpture, observation of the stars, hieroglyphic writing)—suspected of being inspired by the Devil—were forbidden, and those who took part in them were mercilessly hunted down.

The figure of Diego de Landa (1524–79), the first bishop of Yucatán, stands out clearly from the small group of early chroniclers. His *Relación de las Cosas de Yucatán* is our fullest source of information on the 16th-century Maya. Even though, as a man of the cloth, he felt compelled vigorously to denounce many of the Maya customs, his overall conclusions were not entirely negative. Landa often expressed admiration for Maya civilization and for the people, who displayed such Christian virtues as courage, willpower, temperance, and mutual cooperation. He could see they were not savages, but civilized beings who tended their fields with care, planted trees, built fine houses thatched with straw, and created dazzling white cities. At the heart of these cities stood temples surrounded by vast squares; beyond these were the houses of the princes and priests, then those of the more important citizens; while right on the outskirts lived the common folk.

Diego de Landa, dedicated ethnographer and zealous inquisitor, is a paradoxical figure. No one showed greater interest in the Maya and their customs, yet in 1562 he ruthlessly repressed an Indian religious revival, tracking down, torturing, and burning its followers.

Fascinated by the Splendor of the Ancient Sites, Landa Lost Himself in Conjecture

The ruined cities that Landa visited were even more beautiful. He remarked that "this country, although it is a good land, is not at present such as it appears to have been in the prosperous time, when so many and such remarkable buildings were built." In Izamal one of the buildings attracted special attention, and he accompanied his description of it with an annotated sketch. In Tihoo, where the city of Mérida was founded in 1542, he drew a brief plan of an architectural complex reminiscent of the Nunnery Quadrangle in Uxmal.

In addition to the buildings, there were the stelae with their carved inscriptions, like the ones he admired in Mayapán, 120 years after the city had been abandoned. He also described Chichén Itzá and its principal monuments, including the famous Sacred Cenote, or Well of Sacrifice. Landa puzzled over the number of ruined sites and constructed various theories. Perhaps the chiefs wanted to keep their subjects busy, or was building a way of worshiping their gods? Perhaps the location of the cities was

"They received us with their usual cries and hailed down on us stones thrown by hand or with slings, arrows, and spears, wounding several of our party. We well knew that the enemy had not dared to meet us in open country, and although we could have taken a different route, I was afraid of appearing cowardly in passing by without teaching these Mexicans a good lesson."

Letter from Hernán
Cortés to Charles V
of Spain

changed frequently. In any case, the abundance of good-quality materials must have helped the builders in their task. When he questioned local Indians about the stelae in the coastal town of Dzilán, they still knew that "they were accustomed to erect one of these stones every twenty years, which is the number which they use in counting their cycles." In Izamal, on the other hand, no one could remember who had built the dozen or so most remarkable buildings. Showing much good sense, Landa judged that "these buildings have not been constructed by other nations than the Indians; and this is seen from the naked stone men made modest by long girdles which they called in their language *ex* as well as from other devices which the Indians wear."

What Landa Did Not Know Was That the Northern Yucatán Was Only the Tip of the Iceberg

At the time of its greatest splendor, toward the end of the 8th century, the area of Maya civilization extended over the whole peninsula, including the present-day state of Chiapas in Mexico, the region of the Petén in Guatemala, the western part of Honduras, and the north of El Salvador. After the

Although the two images above illustrate episodes from the Aztec conquest, they apply just as well to the conquest of the Maya lands. The clash of two armies (left) also represents the clash of two civilizations— different uniforms and weapons, different tactics. The troop of native bearers following Cortés (right) are from defeated, and therefore "domesticated" tribes. The natives are using a strap around their foreheads to carry the conquerors' burdens, a method common among traditional peoples of Mesoamerica even today.

collapse of the Classic civilization in the 9th century, most of the Maya lands returned to tropical forest and were only sporadically repopulated. For centuries the cities, lying buried in the undergrowth, remained a secret. Their rediscovery, which did not really begin until the late 18th century, was not completed until the late 20th century. First the country itself had to be explored, and this took time, not only because traveling through the forest was dangerous and difficult, but also because the lowlands of Chiapas, Belize, and the Petén held few attractions for either conquerors or colonizers: no rich mineral deposits, little exploitable work force, and a hostile environment. The missionaries were the only ones who dared brave this "green hell," in search of souls to save.

In 1525, however, Cortés crossed the southern Maya lands, from Tabasco to Honduras. Disturbing rumors were circulating about the conduct of his subordinates in Honduras, so the conquistador decided to go there to discover the truth for himself. He gathered 140 Spanish soldiers, 300 Indians as fighters and bearers, 150 horses, a herd of pigs, food supplies, and ammunition.

The journey took nearly six months. First, they had to tackle the swamps of Tabasco, which could often be crossed only by building roads and bridges; then there was the forest, where it was so easy to get lost; and finally there were the daunting mountain ranges, whose precipices claimed the lives of many men and horses. The Spaniards had to rely on the local inhabitants to keep them supplied with food and to show them the way. Yet when they reached the villages, they were often deserted, sometimes even burned to the ground. Fearing the white men, the Indians had fled, and in spite of his protestations that he had no evil intentions towards them, Cortés had the greatest difficulty in persuading them to come back.

One of the most significant points on this journey was the town of Tayasal, built on the largest island of Lake Petén Itzá (in today's Guatemala). It was the

Before the arrival of the conquistadors, horses were unknown in America. During the early battles, when the Indians saw armed cavalry charging towards them, they thought each man and his mount were a single creature, a terrifying form of centaur. To give it a name, they referred to the largest animal they knew; for the Aztecs of the Highlands this was the deer, and for the Lowland Maya it was the tapir.

capital of the Itzá people, the most powerful Maya group in the region. Much impressed by the mass that Cortés celebrated with great pomp and ceremony, "with singing accompanied by trombones and oboes," Canek, their chief, declared he would destroy his own idols and asked the Spaniards to leave him a cross. Cortés also entrusted to him a wounded horse: "The lord promised to take care of it, though I have no idea what he did with it...." Only a century later was its fate discovered.

The Tapir—Horse of Tayasal—Was Smashed to Pieces, a Victim of the Zeal of the Franciscans

In 1618 two Franciscans, Urbita and Fuensalida, who were working as missionaries in Tayasal, found Cortés' horse erected as a statue in one of the main temples of the city; it was shown sitting on the ground just like a human, in a position quite alien to the equine species. After Cortés' departure the Indians had tried to look after it by offering it meat and flowers —the kind of treatment usually reserved for important citizens. The poor creature, as one might imagine, did not survive. The Maya worshiped it by the name of Tzimín Chac, from Tzimín, meaning tapir (the animal most similar to the horse in their experience), and Chac, god of

After 1519 Cortés' life became linked with the history of the conquest of Mexico. Landing on the beaches of Cempoala on 21 April 1519, Cortés received envoys from the Aztec ruler Moctezuma before setting out for the high Mexican plateau. He concluded an alliance with the republic of Tlaxcala and massacred the population of Cholula before continuing his march. When the Aztec capital, Tenochtitlán, fell on 13 August 1521, it was no more than a pile of ruins and corpses. This event sounded the death knell for Mexico as a whole. By 1523 the south and west had been completely defeated by the Spanish.

rain and thunder. At the sight of this idol Father Urbita, seized by holy rage, picked up a large stone and smashed it to pieces. The crowd of worshipers began to shout menacingly, and it seemed inevitable that he would be lynched, until Father Fuensalida saved the situation by preaching at the top of his voice.

Refusing to accept defeat, the holy fathers returned to Tayasal the following year, but they were again rejected by the Itzá priests.

In 1622 Father Delgado Arrived in Tayasal, Accompanied by Eighty Converted Indians. They Were Joyfully Received...and Immediately Sacrificed

In defiance of instructions from the Spanish crown, a Captain Mirones obtained permission from the governor of the Yucatán to mount an expedition against the Itzá. He set up camp in a village halfway between Mérida and Tayasal while he gathered the necessary forces, but his harsh treatment of the native population caused his downfall, as well as that of his companions. While they were celebrating mass, the Indians burst into the church, tore out the hearts of all the Spaniards, and set fire to the village before vanishing back into the forest.

These setbacks discouraged further expeditions for another seventy years. In 1692 Martín de Ursúa, the new governor of the Yucatán, realized that the strength of the Itzá lay in their isolation. This would have to be overcome if they were to be brought to reason and to the true faith. So he built a road intended to link Cauich (Campeche) with Lake Petén Itzá.

Long before it had been completed, a Father Avendaño used it, making the rest of his journey through the forest and finally reaching the lake in January 1696. Once again the king, Canek, and his counselors were asked to swear allegiance to the Spanish crown and to be converted. After much discussion, the Maya gave their response. According to

This 1563 map, in which the west lies at the top, shows that by this date maritime exploration of the continent was considerably advanced, though very little was known about the interior. The Greater Antilles, the first lands to be discovered, are shown in great detail and in their actual form. But even though the coastline is drawn quite accurately, the overall shape of Mexico and Central America leaves something to be desired.

their prophecies, the time was not yet right for them to abandon their gods: "Come back in four months' time, and then we'll see…."

On their return Avendaño and his companions tried to retrace their route, but after wandering

aimlessly in the forest for weeks on end, half dead
with exhaustion and hunger, they were astonished to
come upon a group of ruined buildings.

Although he was very weak, the priest clambered up
the pyramids and from their summits gazed down
upon dwellings "like unto a convent with their little
cloisters, and many dwelling-rooms, all of them
thatched…and whitened within with plaster." His
description of the ruins he saw there seems to fit the
site of Tikal. In the same year a small expedition
traveling down the Usumacinta River discovered
another great ruined city, which later became known
as Yaxchilán (southern Mexico).

To Put an End to Itzá Resistance, Governor Ursúa Resorted to Drastic Measures

In January 1696 two military detachments that had
been sent to the lake were forced to beat a retreat in
the face of Indian hostility. It was now clear that the
Indians would never be defeated without a major
deployment of troops. For over a year the Spanish
prepared for the final assault. Carpenters joined the
ranks to build a galley and canoes to carry the soldiers
to the island.

The city fell early in the morning of 13 March
1697. Panic-stricken at the sound of explosions, the
inhabitants threw themselves into the lake and tried
to swim across it. The Spaniards spent the rest of the
day smashing idols in the deserted city, and by
evening Ursúa had decided where the church should
be built: on the ruins of the great temple. Two
centuries after Christopher Columbus' discovery of
the continent, the conquest of the Maya lands was
finally complete.

This long and difficult process left the Spanish little
time to investigate the historical remains of the Maya
or to take any interest in their significance. Cortés
marched straight past important sites without even
realizing they were there, while Father Avendaño's
finds and the discovery of Yaxchilán were quite

Petrus Aluaradus,
de Mendozza in d
Remi

n dem Landbogt in new Hispanien Antonio
Sibolla geschickt wurde/ der wirdt fast mit allem
on den Califeanern erschlagen.

XXII

The peoples of Mesoamerica were conquered with astonishing rapidity by a handful of Spaniards; the power of the Aztecs was destroyed within two years, and the various kingdoms of Guatemala submitted to Pedro de Alvarado, one of Cortés' lieutenants, after only fifteen months. Certain regions, however, such as the Petén, were only finally defeated in the late 17th century. Others, having initially been conquered and pacified, subsequently rose up; these included the Yucatán and New Galicia (the present-day state of Jalisco, six hundred miles west of Mexico City). It was there that Pedro de Alvarado, called to the aid of fellow Spaniards, met his death in 1541, when the Indians, entrenched on a hilltop, rained down a hail of rocks on the Spanish infantry and cavalry.

unexpected, isolated events that had no immediate outcome. The accounts written by the discoverers of these ruins remained unheeded until they were unearthed centuries later. This was true, for example, in the case of the fascinating report on the ruins of Copán (Honduras), written in 1576 by Diego García de Palacio, judge to the supreme court of Guatemala (see p. 130). Even though the report was addressed to the king of Spain, the ruins it described were to remain hidden for another two and a half centuries.

In 1746 Father Antonio de Solis arrived in Santo Domingo de Palenque with his brothers, their wives, and a swarm of nephews. Looking for new lands to cultivate, the family wandered into the forest…and stumbled across ruined "stone houses." They were the first people from the Old World to set foot, amazed, in one of the most impressive of all Maya sites.

CHAPTER II

ARTISTS AND ADVENTURERS

In the foreground of this *Picturesque View of the Courtyard in the Palace of Palenque* Jean-Frédéric de Waldeck shows a gaping pot-hunter's pit. He wrote that the "dreadful sound" of the wind in the trees clinging to the tower gave rise to the belief that the place was haunted.

Antonio de Solis had been sent to Palenque by his bishop. In the rural area of Chiapas the only building materials were cob and thatch, and only a few churches were built of stone. One can imagine, therefore, the surprise of the priest's family at the sight of the stone monuments there. Since then, every visitor to the site has shared their wonder.

Palenque occupies a special position in the history of the exploration of Maya sites. Although most of them were "discovered" in the 20th century, it soon became clear that many had already been visited by missionaries, soldiers, or officials. Archives often contain evidence of such visits, after which the sites fell once more into complete oblivion. Palenque was an exception to this rule. Because the ruins discovered by Father de Solis were easily accessible and well preserved (most of the buildings still had their roofs), right from the beginning they were visited by a constant stream of inquisitive travelers, scholars, and tourists.

While Still a Student, Ramón Ordonez y Aguiar Heard of the Discovery of Palenque

In 1773, by now an adult accepted into holy orders, Ordonez informed the governor of Guatemala, Don José Estachería, of the existence of the ruins. In 1784 Estachería sent to the site a local official, José Antonio Calderón, who produced a rather dry report, listing over 220 buildings, including 18 palaces, 22 other large edifices, and 168 houses. He made the strange, and completely false, assertion that these buildings were arranged along streets.

This is one of the earliest known drawings of a panel from the Temple of the Sun in Palenque (above). When it is compared with a more recent and accurate version (above right), it becomes clear that the 18th-century artist, Juan Muñoz, was incapable of understanding most of the motifs. Though he has recognized the shield and spears, for example, he completely misinterpreted the jaguar mask below them.

Comparing the two drawings more closely, we find that the small kneeling gods, who support the main figures wearing strange Chinese-style braids, have also been significantly altered.

In these late-18th-century sketches by architect Antonio Bernasconi, showing the Temples of the Cross and the Sun (below), the ground plans and cross-sections of the buildings are rather well done. The roof combs, however, which were unknown in European architecture, have been omitted.

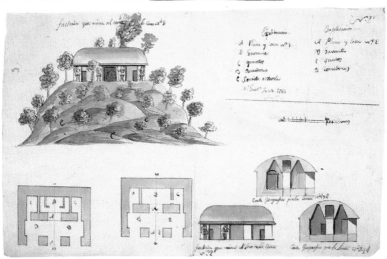

José Castañeda's view of the Palace of Palenque, an architectural complex of about 330 x 260 feet, built over a period of nearly 120 years. The first buildings, dating from the 7th century, were arranged around three courtyards. Vaulted structures were later added around them; they were composed of two porticoes separated by a central wall, one open to the exterior, the other to the courtyards.

In 1785 the governor sent the architect Antonio Bernasconi to Palenque. His report included a plan and estimated the extent of the site, which was contained within a circle "six leagues and a thousand Castilian varas" in circumference. It was illustrated with architectural drawings, mainly elevations and sections through vaults. In his conclusion Bernasconi indicated that the city had not been destroyed by a volcanic eruption or an earthquake, but had simply fallen into ruin as it was gradually abandoned by the inhabitants.

The King of Spain Demanded Samples from the Site, and To Satisfy His Whim del Río Systematically Ransacked Palenque

The file on Palenque was now sufficiently full and detailed to be submitted to the king of Spain, who was known to have a keen interest in such matters. Before coming to the throne, Charles III had been ruler in Naples, where he had financed the first excavations in Pompeii; he had even established an important collection of classical archaeology. After consulting Juan-Bautista Muñoz, his official specialist on the history of the New World, the king ordered the government of Guatemala to undertake a more thorough investigation of the site. Bernasconi, who had just died, was replaced by Captain Antonio del Río. He arrived at the site known as the Casas de Piedra, or Houses of Stone, on 5 May 1786, but the forest was so dense he could see nothing. At his request the authorities employed seventy-nine Indians armed with axes to clear the undergrowth from around the ruins.

Del Río followed the royal instructions to the letter, describing and measuring the monuments, and removing as many relics as possible. He tore out a stucco head here, a limestone panel covered with carved

Waldeck's engraving shows a king framed by two defeated enemies. All the details —from the physical type and costume of the figures to the objects held by the king —are inaccurate.

glyphs there. A stone throne was left unsteady when he removed one of its carved legs; he mutilated a stucco inscription by hacking out the best-preserved glyphs. He left gaping holes everywhere, in the walls of the palace buildings and in the temples; and in the process he often discovered votive offerings of pottery and stone-carved weapons. The fruits of this pillage were sent to the Royal Museum of Natural History in Madrid.

The Spanish Found It Impossible To Believe That Such Impressive Architecture Could Be the Work of the Natives Alone

Del Río's report was not published until 1822, in London and in English, illustrated with engravings by Jean-Frédéric de Waldeck. For del Río, as for many of his contemporaries, the only great civilization was the classical. Because he admired the buildings of Palenque, he was convinced that the Greeks and Romans must have had a hand in their construction: "I do not take upon myself to assert that these conquerors [the Romans] did actually land in this country, but there is reasonable ground for hazarding a conjecture that some inhabitants of that polished nation did visit these regions; and that from much intercourse the natives might have embraced during their stay an idea of the arts as a reward for their hospitality." Nevertheless, del Río observed elsewhere that "the identity of the ancient inhabitants of Yucatán and Palenque is, in my opinion, evidently proved by the strong analogy of their customs, building, and acquaintance with the arts."

Twenty years later Palenque was

The carving on the back of this throne shows King Pacal's mother presenting him with a crown. For some reason, Waldeck thought the main figure was a queen. Later, the "queen" was renamed the "Ethiopian woman."

visited by Captain Guillermo Dupaix, who had been instructed by the new king of Spain, Charles IV, to carry out a survey of all the ruins in Mexico dating from before the Conquest. Of Austrian descent, Dupaix had received an excellent classical education in Italy before making his career in the Spanish army, first in Spain, then in Mexico. Between 1805 and 1807 he undertook three voyages of archaeological exploration, and it was during the third that he visited the Maya ruins of Toniná and Palenque. He was accompanied by José Luciano Castañeda, a Mexican draftsman whose engravings are much "beautified," in the style of the period. Even though Castañeda's work is infinitely superior to the drawings executed by his

During their voyage of archaeological exploration, Dupaix and Castañeda frequently stopped to draw anything they came across that was picturesque or beautiful —this bridge on the road to Palenque, for example.

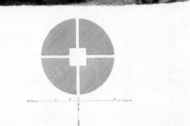

predecessors, his rather fanciful copies of bas-reliefs and, especially, of glyphs often reveal that the artist did not understand the images he was trying to reproduce. Dupaix, on the other hand, was an excellent observer. He noted that in all the Maya sites the permanent structures were built of stone rather than brick (Comalcalco is the only exception), that the lintels were made of wood, and that two modeling techniques were used for the stucco bas-reliefs, etc.

Dupaix' reports and Castañeda's drawings did not come to light until well after the Mexican war of independence, and it was not until 1828 that a Frenchman named Henri Baradère obtained the documents from the Mexican government. Dupaix'

Although the ruins generally looked like misshapen mounds, Dupaix and Castañeda tried to suggest the form of the original structure with simplified sketches.

Dibujo de Del Rio.

Three drawings of a stucco relief from the Palace of Palenque. A teacher knows when two pupils have been copying each other when the same mistakes appear in the work of each. This is also true when we compare a drawing attributed by Waldeck to del Río (far left) with another attributed to Castañeda (above). In both cases the head of the serpent has been transformed into a flower; the woman's hair has been imaginatively rearranged; the axe blade has become a ribbon; and the pedestal decorated with heads is pure invention. Waldeck's painting (left) shows that he found it difficult to escape the influence of these earlier interpretations.

description of his travels did not appear until 1830, in one of the volumes published by Lord Edward Kingsborough. In 1834 the two huge volumes of *Antiquités mexicaines* (*Mexican Antiquities*) were printed in Paris. In this publication, which is very characteristic of the period, Dupaix' text is printed primarily as the basis for a series of

After Copán was abandoned in the 9th century, the river wore its way into the very heart of the city, exposing a section over 90 feet in height where areas of wall, stuccoed floors, and broad tunnels could be seen. Galindo (left) thought it was a huge wall pierced by windows—hence the name "Las Ventanas," by which the site was known for a long time.

reflections by a number of distinguished scholars; Alexandre Lenoir, for example, an archaeologist and specialist on French monuments, submitted an essay entitled "Comparison of the Ancient Monuments of Mexico with Those of Egypt, India, and the Rest of the Ancient

World," while Charles Farcy published a "Discourse on Two Questions Submitted to the Historical Congress of Europe, Being: to Discuss…the Value of Documents Relating to the History of America, and to Decide Whether There is Any Link Between the Languages of the Various American Tribes and Those of Africa and India." It is amusing to note that while scholars were unable to extricate themselves from the influence of classical culture, more straightforward, less educated minds were displaying far more common sense. Dupaix was one of the first of his generation to conceive of a native American civilization.

The Son of Actors, Juan Galindo Left His Native Ireland for America in Search of Adventure at the Age of Sixteen

By 1827 Galindo was in Guatemala, working for the Central American Federation, which was at that time having great difficulty in imposing itself on its various member states. Appointed colonel, Galindo became military governor of the Petén, and it was in this context that he took a trip to Palenque in 1831. In the same year he visited the ruins of the island of Topoxté, on Lake Yaxhá, and in 1834 he spent a month in Copán. He described and sketched the monuments there; he drew up a plan of the site and a map of the region, and carried out excavations, notably of a vaulted tomb.

Galindo observed, as Landa had, nearly two centuries before, that the clothes worn by the people modeled or carved in the ruins were very similar to those of the native inhabitants of the country. From this he concluded that the Indians who had built these ancient cities were of the same race as the modern Indians. But, he continued, they must have predated the

On the road and in the villages through which he passed, Galindo enjoyed making sketches of the Indians and half-castes wearing their typical costumes.

Aztecs, because if they had been contemporaries, the Aztecs would surely have borrowed from the Maya their hieroglyphic script, which they were the only people in America to have developed.

At this time the geographical society in Paris (Société de Géographie) enjoyed considerable prestige, and travelers and explorers sent letters from all over the world, hoping to have them printed in the society's bulletin. Galindo submitted a total of thirty-two, many of which were published. He also wrote a report on each of the countries of Central America and drew several maps. His map of Central America was awarded a silver medal, but sadly the society was never able to present it to him; after the defeat of the federal troops, to whose ranks he belonged, Galindo tried to escape, in the thick of the civil war, accompanied by two dragoons and a servant. But he was recognized while passing through a village, and the four men were massacred with machetes. He was thirty-eight years old.

In the History of the Discovery of the Maya, Waldeck Ranks as the First Great Artist and the Last of the Great Adventurers

Jean-Frédéric Maximilien, Comte de Waldeck, born in Vienna (or in Prague, according to some sources) of Austrian descent, always created an immediate impression with his great height and bulk and his clear, deep voice, which he knew how to use to advantage. He was well aware of his skill as a raconteur, and in company he always did his best to

"The method of traveling in the interior of Yucatán is similar to that used in the Far East. You are carried by men in a covered litter called a coche (pronounced 'co-chay')...."

attract attention. In spite of his white hair and beard, even at the age of 102 he looked only seventy.

A talented artist who was never short of work, he claimed to have studied painting in the Paris studio of Jacques-Louis David—though it may have been that of Pierre Prud'hon, unless, of course, it was in Berlin. And in any case, one wonders how he ever found time to study, for Waldeck lived life to the fullest.

In 1785 he had sailed with the explorer François Levaillant as far as the Cape of Good Hope and

"Once you have grown used to this form of palanquin, you will prefer it to riding a horse because you are sheltered from the rain and sun and can read and sleep at leisure."
Jean-Frédéric de Waldeck
Voyage pittoresque, 1838

Romantic Realism

In this painting Waldeck has altered the landscape so that the mountain in the background looks like a larger replica of the Temple of the Cross and of its pyramid, covered with vegetation. He probably based his version on the equally incorrect view by Frederick Catherwood. Like of most of the buildings in Palenque, the temple supports a roof comb, or parapet, shaped as an inverted V and pierced by many openings intended to lighten its weight and create less wind resistance. Very little remains of its stuccoed decoration. The huts visible at the foot of the pyramid are the quarters Waldeck had built so he could live there.

A Picturesque View

I t was one of Waldeck's usual tricks to adapt the landscapes he was painting—almost as if he felt the background "decor," constructed centuries earlier by the Maya, could only be understood through such romantically inspired modifications. An example of this is his *Picturesque View and Elevation in Oils of the Ruined Facade of the Palace of Palenque.* The figures and animals Waldeck introduced into the foreground of his picturesque views were omitted in the 1866 publication *Monuments anciens du Mexique* (*Ancient Monuments of Mexico*).

explored southern Africa. He was no stranger to the army, either, and was once heard to confide to a young woman that he had been involved in forty-two revolutions. He volunteered to fight in Bonaparte's Italian campaigns and took part in the siege of Toulon. His great admiration for the general took Waldeck next to Egypt. His vast stock of anecdotes included one that revealed how his talent for pastiches—uncharitable tongues might say for forgery—reached the ears of Bonaparte himself. When they met, the general asked Waldeck to copy his famous signature on a folded sheet of paper, and when he had finished, our hero unfolded the paper and read at the top of the document the words: "Condemned to three months' imprisonment in Vincennes." Bonaparte was said to have taken pity on Waldeck, however, leaving him in prison only two weeks.

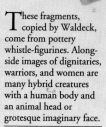

These fragments, copied by Waldeck, come from pottery whistle-figurines. Alongside images of dignitaries, warriors, and women are many hybrid creatures with a human body and an animal head or grotesque imaginary face.

One of his best, though most tragic, tales described how, to escape the Turks, he had fled Aswan and crossed the Dongola Desert, his four comrades dying one by one from exhaustion and disease. Half dead himself, after four months of deprivation in the face of every conceivable danger, he reached the Portuguese settlements and safety.

On another evening he might be asked to recount the sequel to this adventure, when he had sailed the Indian Ocean in a privateer, in the company of Surcouf, the so-called "patriotic pirate." Some listeners were regaled with tales of how he had "helped Chile to achieve independence"; his audience would shiver as he told of the skirmishes and ambushes in which Waldeck and his companion Lord Cochrane had escaped death a hundred times over; and they would laugh at his description of the cowardly mercenaries who had accompanied the two counts on their Chilean adventure.

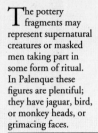

In 1819 Waldeck visited Guatemala, and three years later, in London, he did some engravings to illustrate del Río's report, based on the drawings of a Guatemalan architect, Ricardo Almendaríz, who had accompanied del Río. In a letter to the Société de Géographie he summed up this decisive experience: "The publication, in London, of del Río's very incomplete work was partly due to me; it was brought from America in 1822 by a Doctor Mac Quy, who showed it to me; he sold it to the London publisher Henry Berthoud, and I was asked to do the plates for it, as you can see from the initials J.-F. W. written at the bottom of most of them; one even carries my full name. From the moment I first saw the pen-and-ink drawings in this work, I suspected that they were less than faithful to the originals and I began to cherish a secret desire to go and draw them for myself."

In 1825, aged nearly sixty and married for a second time, Waldeck seemed to be showing signs of wanting to "settle down"; he accepted a post as engineer at a silver mine in Michoacán, western Mexico. But he soon found life there far too dreary for his liking, and,

The pottery fragments may represent supernatural creatures or masked men taking part in some form of ritual. In Palenque these figures are plentiful; they have jaguar, bird, or monkey heads, or grimacing faces.

without waiting for his contract to expire, he moved to Mexico City. There his interest in antiquities grew; he drew the objects on display in the National Museum (published in 1827 under the title *Collection of Mexican Antiquities*) and he visited the sites.

He was still eager to fulfill his old dream—to draw the monuments of Palenque—and a subscription was launched, with the support of the vice president of the Mexican Republic, to finance the expedition. But the money was slow to arrive, and after a year Waldeck lost patience, pocketed the funds that had so far been collected—one third of the amount originally required—and arrived in Palenque in May 1832.

Waldeck Drew to His Heart's Content

Living in dangerous and uncomfortable conditions in a hut at the foot of the Temple of the Cross, Waldeck produced plans and elevations of the buildings, as well as drawings of the stone carvings and stucco reliefs, and paintings of many picturesque landscapes showing the ruins against a backdrop of forest and peopled by figures. He had to endure the heat, the mosquitoes, and the damp, and he had to watch the rain falling in torrents for days on end, with no one to talk to but the few half-castes who helped him to clear the undergrowth from the ruins. To withstand all this, at the age of sixty-seven, he must have had an exceptional constitution, a great deal of courage, and above all an inexhaustible devotion to his work, which he was able to pursue thanks to the generosity of Lord Kingsborough.

In July 1853 Barnum exhibited young twins in London as "Aztecs." Waldeck compared the profile of the boy with a Palenque relief to demonstrate that the exhibition was a fake.

This copy of the Beau Relief from Palenque (right) is of inestimable value, because although it is treated in Waldeck's usual style, which owes as much to the Greeks and Egyptians as to the Maya, the original is today almost completely destroyed. The king is seated on a two-headed jaguar throne similar to the one on which Pacal is sitting in the Oval Panel (see p. 31). Incongruous elements—a marimba, cuneiform characters—have crept into the glyphs on the right-hand side of the panel; these are entirely the product of Waldeck's imagination.

After Palenque he went on to Mayapán, Toniná, and Uxmal. In 1866 fifty-six lithographs by Waldeck were used to illustrate a text by Brasseur de Bourbourg: *Monuments anciens du Mexique, Palenque et autres ruines de l'ancienne civilisation du Mexique*

(Ancient Monuments of Mexico, Palenque, and Other Ruins of the Ancient Civilizations of Mexico).

As a man of the late 18th century (he was thirty-four in 1800), Waldeck was convinced, as were many others, that the great civilization whose ruins he was drawing had its roots in the ancient world. In studying Maya art, he was therefore on the lookout for evidence of Hindu, Hebrew, Greek, and Egyptian influence. As such evidence did not exist, he found none—or, rather, whenever he "found" such "evidence," it seemed insufficient, so he was careful to make surreptitious adjustments to reality in order to make it correspond more closely to his convictions. Waldeck's oeuvre is in the image of its creator: seductive, romantic in flavor, and a trifle misleading.

After eleven years in Mexico Waldeck returned to Paris, where he published his *Voyage pittoresque et archéologique dans la province d'Yucatán* in 1838. It describes the Maya ruins in great detail, but much space is also devoted to modern-day inhabitants of the Yucatán. At the age of eighty-four Waldeck married again, this time a young Englishwoman of seventeen, who bore him a son, Gaston. In his Montmartre apartment on the Rue des Martyrs he lived quietly, surrounded by his paintings and souvenirs. He continued to write articles, to paint, and to exhibit. Even the manner of his death, at the age of 110, is the stuff of legend; he is said to have tripped while turning to look at a pretty woman on the street.

The Greco-Egyptian style developed by Waldeck can be clearly seen in his reconstruction of one of the statues on the facade of the Magician's Pyramid in Uxmal (left). The artist was probably inspired by one of the statuettes (about 20 inches—not 10 feet!—tall) that decorate the facades of the Nunnery Quadrangle.

The foreground of this picturesque view of a building in the Palace of Palenque is occupied by the struggle between a snake and an iguana. The keyhole shape of the arched doorway was developed by the Maya to lessen the weight of the roof. To the right of the entrance one of the stucco medallions is depicted as being still intact; today, all that remains is the frame. Waldeck amused himself by copying the graffiti and inscriptions left by previous visitors to the site; on the right is the signature of a certain Guilhou, who visited the ruins in 1832, while on the left a lengthy inscription by a French doctor named Corroy informs posterity that in that same year he, his wife, and two children were visiting Palenque for the third time.

In 1805 John Stephens, the man who is considered the true "discoverer" of the Maya, was born into a well-to-do New England family. Though he was not the first to visit the sites of Central America, it was he who introduced them to a wider public through his writings. With Stephens, the era of wild romantic imaginings came to an end.

CHAPTER III

THE AGE OF THE SCHOLARS

As there are no rivers in the Yucatán, water has always been collected from cenotes (from the Maya word *dzonot*): natural sinkholes formed by the collapse of part of the limestone layer. The water is often deep underground; in Bolonchen, for example, the Indians had to build a gigantic ladder so they could climb down to it.

At the age of twenty-nine, having completed his law studies, Stephens boarded a ship for Europe and the Near East. On his return he published his travel writings: *Incidents of Travel in Egypt, Arabia, Petraea, and the Holy Land*, followed by *Incidents of Travel in Greece, Turkey, Russia, and Poland*. In 1836, encouraged by the success of these works, he was planning to set off once more in search of material for a third title in the series when he met in London a young English architect, Frederick Catherwood, who was an excellent draftsman and also an avid traveler. The young men got along well, and while they were talking, Catherwood drew his friend's attention to del Río's report, illustrated by Waldeck's engravings.

Stephens Sensed That a Description of the Ruins of this Exotic and Virtually Unknown Civilization Could Arouse Immense Public Interest

On his return to New York Stephens found a copy of Waldeck's *Voyage pittoresque* in a bookshop, and the artistic quality of the lithographs convinced him of the unique beauty of the ruins. He spoke of this to Catherwood, who traveled to join him. However, civil war was raging among the supporters of the Central American Federation (which until 1838 included Guatemala, Honduras, El Salvador, Nicaragua, and Costa Rica), nationalist factions, and rebel Indians. It was out of the question for Stephens and Catherwood to travel around the area as tourists. Then an opportunity presented itself; the new United States chargé d'affaires to Central America died suddenly, just as he was about to take up the post, and Stephens put himself forward as a replacement.

"We lived in the ruined palace of their kings; we went up to their desolate temples and fallen altars; and wherever we moved we saw the evidences of their taste, their skill in arts, their wealth, and power. In the midst of desolation and ruin we looked back to the past, cleared away the gloomy forest, and fancied every building perfect, with its terraces and pyramids, its sculptured and painted ornaments, grand, lofty, and imposing."

John L. Stephens,
Incidents of Travel in Central America, Chiapas, and Yucatán, 1841

The name of the so-called Governor's Palace in Uxmal no doubt evokes something of its true function. The building is composed of three parts. The facade of the main body of the structure has seven doorways, three of which give access to the principal chamber; above the central doorway is the image of a prince seated on a throne. The two smaller wings were originally separated from the central building by vaulted passages, though, as we can see from Catherwood's engraving, these were later blocked up.

The Castillo

At the end of the 10th century Chichén Itzá grew more metropolitan and became home to many foreigners, some of whom were surely the Toltecs of Central Mexico, led by the legendary "feathered serpent" Quetzalcoatl. The latter had been expelled from Tula (north of Mexico City) by a rival faction. The "Castillo," or castle, as the Spanish conquerors called it, shows the architectural innovations of the time, some of them based on the theme of the "feathered serpent." On each face of the pyramid, as well as on the main facade, the ramps were designed to resemble the bodies of snakes, with their heads resting at the foot of the slope. One of these heads is visible in this view by Catherwood. The main entrance to the temple has three openings, each formed by two serpent-shaped columns. Their jaws are at ground level, the bodies form the column shafts, and the tails support the lintel.

The Arch at Labná

In the Maya sites of the Puuc region of Yucatán a complex made up of four buildings arranged around a courtyard is called a "quadrangle." In Labná two quadrangles lying side by side are connected by a monumental vaulted doorway, which visitors often mistake for some form of triumphal arch. There is a room on either side of the passageway, and above the doors to these rooms are hut-shaped niches which once held stucco statues. The "huts" look like miniature versions of the thatched houses that can be seen in Yucatecan villages today. They can also be found in Uxmal, carved on the south building of the Nunnery Quadrangle, which was so named by the Spanish because they thought it resembled a convent.

Tulum, in the Yucatán

Stephens and Catherwood are seen here taking measurements of the Temple of Frescoes in Tulum. This small town on the edge of the Caribbean, built shortly before the Conquest, was surrounded by a defensive wall. Most of the houses were arranged on either side of a main street, while the most important buildings were grouped together at the center of the site. Two of the temples in Tulum contained well-preserved frescoes painted in blue-green on a black background; the mythological subjects include Chac, the rain god, and the goddess Ixchel, who was the focus of a very important cult at the time of the Spaniards' arrival. Pilgrimages were made to her shrine on the island of Cozumel, about 30 miles northeast of Tulum.

Itzamná, in Izamal

One of the buildings in Izamal was decorated with a huge, well-preserved stucco mask, over 6.5 feet high, of the old fire god, Itzamná. Though this form of decoration was widely used in Maya architecture, this is one of the only examples to have survived exposure to the open air, and for this reason it came as a great surprise to Stephens. To enliven the scene and to emphasize the dramatic aspects of the giant wall with its strange mask, Catherwood included in his composition a hunter, accompanied by an Indian, chasing a jaguar, which can be seen hiding in the shadow by the wall. It was in Izamal that Diego de Landa had a Franciscan church and convent built on the site of one of the ruined pyramids of the ancient Maya city.

He was accepted, thanks to his political connections.

The two friends at last set out on a perilous diplomatic and archaeological adventure that was to last nearly ten months. As Catherwood later described it, the adventurer Stephens "combined the pursuit of an elusive government with a more fruitful search for ruined cities." In the course of their long journey Stephens and Catherwood visited Copán, Quiriguá, Toniná, Palenque, and Uxmal. Copán was the site that detained them by far the longest; its buildings and monuments are described and illustrated in great detail.

Stephens' Account of the Expedition, Which Is Both an Adventure Story and an Archaeological Study, Was Enthusiastically Received

Incidents of Travel in Central America, Chiapas, and Yucatán, published in 1841, owed its success primarily to Stephens' narrative skills. Only just over a third of the book deals with archaeology; the bulk is devoted to their adventures (problems with mules, missed meals, unexpected soakings, arrest by soldiers), descriptions of the landscapes, cities, and villages through which they passed and of the people they met, the politics of Central America, and even information about the Conquest and colonial history. Written with humor and sensitivity, the book is the work of a true gentleman.

In contrast to the naive enthusiasm and unbridled speculation of his predecessors, Stephens' descriptions

A mysterious stela stands in the half-darkness behind a brightly lit altar (above). Although he was careful to reproduce the forms accurately, Catherwood sometimes resorted to such dramatic lighting effects to express the feelings of awe and wonder inspired in him, for example, by this group of carvings in Copán. In the engraving on the right he has chosen to show the inscription on the back of a stela.

were more restrained, his interpretations more cautious, and his arguments more clearly argued. He brought to the subject a "modern" perspective; his tone was more convincing, and his judgments were more reliable, because his reflections were always founded on solid knowledge. Stephens knew as much about the history of the Conquest as about the discoveries of his predecessors. He was careful to avoid using the word "Maya" to describe the former inhabitants of the ruins he visited, and, like many of his contemporaries, he wondered about their origins. After weighing various theories, he concluded that the people in question were a native people, characterized by monumental architecture, original sculpture, and a true system of writing. The figures on the "idols"—they were not yet called stelae—were no doubt their leaders. Stephens categorically rejected the elephants that Waldeck had claimed to see carved on the monuments.

Catherwood's Artistic Precision Complemented Stephens' Narrative Rigor, Setting New Standards for the Period

Catherwood's work includes the engraved drawings (of landscapes, ruins, and monuments) that illustrated Stephens' two-volume book, as well as an album of lithographs of the ruins, which was published in London in 1844. The engravings are imbued with charm and poetry, but picturesque qualities are not allowed to dominate at the expense of authenticity. Catherwood made great use of a *camera lucida* to help him reproduce the original proportions accurately. Nevertheless, not everything is perfect. The glyphs, in particular, are rather loosely sketched—though at least there are no additions, such as elephant heads or cuneiform characters.

Stephens and Catherwood had intended to continue their trip by exploring the Yucatán, but Catherwood fell ill in Uxmal, and they were both obliged to return to the United States. In October

In all Maya villages, as here, in Sabachtsché, the well was once the center of women's social life. They met there to draw water, to wash, and to exchange the latest news. Catherwood was sensitive to the biblical echoes of such a scene.

1842 they returned to the Yucatán for a final *Incidents of Travel* book. They stayed there until June of the following year, and their book appeared a few months later.

This time the proportion of the work devoted to archaeology was increased; there are descriptions and drawings of all forty-four of the sites they visited. Catherwood, who was more at ease drawing architectural elevations than artifacts and sculpture, threw himself into the project with enthusiasm, producing some of his best work. The volume on the Yucatán was just as successful as that on Central America had been, and it was reprinted virtually every year throughout the 19th century. Stephens' influence on Maya archaeology was to prove decisive.

"This rancho was distinguished by a well, the sight of which was more grateful to us than that of the best hotel to the traveler in a civilized country. We were scratched with thorns, and smarting with garrapata [tick] bites, and looked forward to the refreshment of a bath. Very soon our horses had the benefit of it, the bath being, in that country, where the currycomb and brush are entirely unknown, the only external refreshment these animals ever get. The well was built by the present owner, and formerly the inhabitants were dependent entirely upon the well at Tabi, six miles distant."

John L. Stephens,
Incidents of Travel in Yucatán, 1843

While Some Explored the Forests of America, Others Rummaged in Libraries for Forgotten Manuscripts

Three types of written work were of interest to researchers: codices (Maya manuscripts written in hieroglyphs) dating from before the arrival of the Spanish, native texts from the post-Conquest period, transcribed in Latin script, and, finally, the chronicles of Spanish conquistadors, churchmen, and officials.

Of the thousands of Maya books, only three have

The *Dresden Codex* is largely made up of almanacs, which, in their simplest form, divide a cycle of 260 days into five groups of 52 days. The images represent the gods who bring good luck on particular days in each group.

survived down to the present day, though the fragment of a fourth was recently discovered. There is a tendency to hold the missionaries uniquely responsible for the disappearance of the Maya manuscripts, but in fact sheer carelessness is often to blame as well. How many of them were collected by the Spanish as objects of curiosity, and kept for a while before being thrown away?

In 1739 Johann Götze, head of the Royal Saxon Library in Dresden, went on a trip to Italy. Traveling through Vienna, he found and bought a hieroglyphic manuscript, known from then on as the *Codex Dresdensis*, or *Dresden Codex*, after the city where it is still kept. It is no coincidence that it should have been found in Vienna, for Charles V of Spain had his residence in this city. In 1519 Cortés had sent from Mexico part of the spoils of his ongoing journey of conquest. Among the treasures were examples of Indian manuscripts, and the *Dresden Codex*, which probably originated in the eastern Yucatán, must have been among them. No one knows through whose hands the manuscript had passed between 1519 and 1739; after that date it lay undisturbed in the archives of the Dresden library for nearly a century, simply being recorded in one catalogue after another.

While still a student at Oxford, Edward King, the young Lord Kingsborough, developed a great enthusiasm for the study of Mexican (non-Maya) manuscripts in the famous Bodleian Library. He noticed that although other native manuscripts still existed, scattered

Maya manuscripts were written on long sheets of paper made from the inner bark of a certain variety of fig tree. The sheets, which could be up to about 22 feet in length, were covered with lime paint, then screen-folded, like an accordion, each page being about twice as tall as it was wide. The hieroglyphs were then inscribed in black or red, and the pictures that accompanied them were drawn in black, occasionally heightened with color or placed on a colored ground.

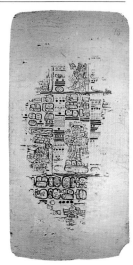

throughout the world, from Rome, Paris, Dresden, and Vienna to Mexico City, there was only a single copy of each one. He also found that the accounts written by explorers were largely unknown. So Kingsborough determined to devote the rest of his life to publishing facsimile copies of as many documents as possible relating to Pre-Columbian Mexico. This would give researchers easy access to the surviving manuscripts, enabling them to make helpful comparisons.

Although several copies of the *Dresden Codex* have been published since then, the "Kingsborough" is still referred to today in order to check certain details that have since disappeared from the original. Kingsborough accompanied his facsimiles with a commentary that today seems rather amusing; he was convinced that the Indians were descended from the Lost Tribes of Israel. His generosity (he financed one of Waldeck's expeditions) and the immensity of the task he had set himself left him a ruined man. Thrown into prison for debt, he fell ill and died, in 1837, at the age of forty-two.

The manuscript known as the *Codex Peresianus* is, in its present state, 57 inches long; it is folded into eleven pages (at least two are missing) written on both sides. On the recto is a series of eleven *katun* ends (7200 days) which provide a framework for historical events and prophecies. The divinities who rule over each *katun* are shown, as well as the rituals that should be performed in their honor. The verso is very badly damaged, but the remains of almanacs, new year's ceremonies, and some form of Maya zodiac can be made out.

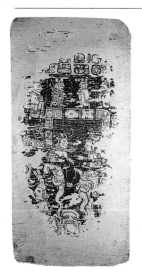

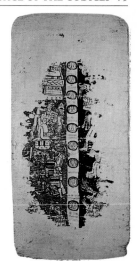

A Second Maya Manuscript Was Found in Paris

In 1859 Léon de Rosny, a young French Orientalist and Americanist, together with some of his colleagues, founded the Société Américaine de France (now the Société des Américanistes). In order to "provide subjects of research for the members of the new association," and to satisfy his passion for deciphering scripts, Rosny began to hunt for manuscripts that might be lying forgotten in private and public collections. The Bibliothèque Nationale had no catalogue of its Mexican manuscripts at the time, so the young man disturbed a great deal of dust, flicking through countless files, until one day, in a wastepaper basket that seemed to contain nothing but discarded scraps, he laid his hands on the second Maya manuscript. He had it photographed and published five years later, as the *Codex Peresianus,* or *Paris Codex.*

The discovery of the third manuscript seems even more fortuitous than that of the other two. Its history is closely linked to one of the most interesting figures in Central American studies, the Abbé C. E. Brasseur de Bourbourg. Born near Dunkirk, in northern France, Brasseur managed to combine his modest priestly duties with research. At a very young age he visited the United States, and then Rome, and the books he read there aroused his curiosity about the New World. At the age of thirty-one he traveled to Mexico, and while on the boat he was lucky enough to meet the French plenipotentiary minister to Mexico. Their friendship soon led to Brasseur's being appointed chaplain to the French Legation, a post that gave him plenty of time to search the archives and storage rooms of the museums. He sometimes escaped from Mexico City itself to visit archaeological sites, but it was above all the Indian languages that fascinated him. In Mexico City he learned Nahuatl, the still-living Aztec tongue, and he discovered in the archives his first Mexican manuscript, which he called the *Codex Chimalpopoca*, after his Nahuatl teacher.

The *Popol Vuh*, which means "Book of Counsel" in Quiché Maya, was so called because whenever they met, the Quiché lords, whose kingdom occupied almost the entire western half of the highlands of Guatemala, would spend much time consulting it about the future.

Abbé Brasseur Proved an Astonishingly Prolific Researcher

The archbishop in Guatemala was sympathetic towards the young French clergyman and offered him the opportunity to follow his double vocation by appointing him priest to the parish of Rabinal, in the heart of Quiché country. There, living with the Indians, he learned the language and discovered enormously important documents— among them the *Popol Vuh*, the epic tale

of the Quiché Maya (both a history and a collection of myths), and the *Rabinal Achi*, one of the few Maya "plays." Soon afterwards he became priest of San Juan Sacatepequez, among the Cakchiquel Indians. Here, too, he found the book of the people's history, the *Memorial de Sololá*. In 1857 he returned to Europe and threw himself into a frenzy of activity. No modern researcher could hope to match the unbridled speed at which his works were published. Between 1857 and 1862 he produced *History of the Civilized Nations of Mexico and Central America*, a translation of the *Popol Vuh*, and *Journey on the Isthmus of Tehuantepec*, not to mention a grammar and vocabulary of the Quiché language. Meanwhile, he discovered one of the most vital manuscripts for the study of the Maya: Diego de Landa's *Relación de las Cosas de Yucatán*, a translation of which he published in 1864.

Supreme Happiness for Abbé Brasseur: A Collector Entrusted Him with a Codex

By 1866, when his report on Palenque, illustrated by Waldeck, was published, Brasseur was a respected expert in the field. In addition to preparing his many publications, he was lecturing on the archaeology of the New World at the Sorbonne, as well as being an active member of many scholarly societies. On a trip to Madrid he visited the Royal Academy of History, where he was introduced to Don Juan de Tro y Ortolano, an eminent collector of ancient manuscripts. The latter showed Brasseur one of his

The publication of a translation of the *Popol Vuh* in Vienna in 1857 went virtually unnoticed. C. E. Brasseur de Bourbourg (opposite, above) attracted more attention with his 1861 version because he provided both the Quiché text and its French translation (opposite, below). The emblem of the twisted snakes on the title page of his version is borrowed from the cover of Stephens' and Catherwood's *Incidents of Travel* of 1843.

The book's frontispiece (left) is a drawing of a pottery incense burner dating from the Post-Classic period (around A.D. 1000). It shows Tlaloc, the Central American god of rain, who was popular with the Maya during this period. He is characterized by his long teeth, which stick out of his curved mouth, and by the rings around his eyes. The artist revealed his origins by treating the eyes in a purely European style.

finest treasures, and the priest recognized in the manuscript some of the characters that had been drawn by Landa, which he had also found in inscriptions from Palenque. Seeing his excitement, the archivist generously offered to lend him the manuscript, which became known as the *Codex Troano*—formed by combining two parts of the owner's name. Brasseur kept it for two and a half years, drew it, studied it, and in 1869 he published it. The original was then returned to Juan de Tro, and on his death six years later the collector's son sold the codex to the archaeological museum in Madrid.

The Suspicious Affair of the Third Codex

The story does not end there. Another Madrid collector, Don Juan Ignacio Miró, sold to the same archaeological museum three pieces of sculpture from Uxmal, along with a manuscript known as the *Codex Cortesiano*. Apparently obtained from the descendants of Hernán Cortés, this was said to be one of three Mexican manuscripts that had been owned by the conquistador.

Léon de Rosny already knew of the existence of such a document, as it had been offered to the Bibliothèque Nationale in Paris, together with photographs of two sheets from the original attached to the offer of sale as a specimen; Rosny had even published one of these. When he heard in 1880 that the Spanish government had acquired the codex, he hurried to Madrid to see it. Once he had a chance to study the manuscript carefully, he noticed that the supposed first page of the *Cortesiano* was in fact the continuation of another text. Intrigued, he examined the document further, and was able to show that it followed on from the last page of the *Codex Troano*. The *Troano* and *Cortesiano* were therefore two parts of the same

The figure with the black-painted body (right) is Ek Chuah, god of trade and cacao (the beans were used as currency), who also has warlike aspects. In his left hand he brandishes a javelin, while in his right he grips a serpent. An axe is buried in his forehead, and his headdress includes a deer's head and a worm. The *Madrid Codex* (also above) is far cruder in style than the *Dresden Codex*. The execution is often clumsy and schematic, and the proportions vary from one figure to the next, because several artists worked on the manuscript.

document, which became the *Codex Tro-Cortesiano*,
known since 1945 as the *Madrid Codex*.

It is a strange tale. In 1864 only two Maya manuscripts were known to exist in the whole world. In
1865 another came on to the market, and in 1872 a
fourth appeared; the two documents were later found
to form part of a single manuscript. It is almost
certain that the original manuscript was cut in half
and sold to two separate collectors, but as the dealer
concerned was careful to preserve his anonymity, the
mystery remains as yet unsolved.

As he grew older, Brasseur allowed his intensely
romantic imagination to get the better of him and he
began to fall prey to curious obsessions. The *Codex
Troano* had first seemed to him to be "a sort of
almanac for the use of rural landowners." Then
it occurred to him that this document, along
with all the other "hieratic" or
"katunic" Maya manuscripts,
described the disappearance of
Atlantis. It came as a revelation
to him: "All my doubts
vanished,
imperceptibly my
uncertainty ceased.
Gradually I
unlocked the
mystery of these
strange images, and at
last the final veil was
drawn away and I began
to read the inscriptions
through from beginning
to end."

When Rosny pointed
out that he was reading the
manuscript back to front, Brasseur was quite
unperturbed. He had no qualms about
declaring, "I have lifted the blue
veil from the sanctuary of Isis."

CENTRAL AMERICA

UXMAL
Magician's Pyramid
(Post-Classic)

ISLAND OF JAINA
An official
(Classic pottery figure)

YUCATÁ

Gulf of Campeche

EDZNÁ Temple

Lowla

MEXICO

TABASCO

TIKAL
Temple of the Jaguar
(Classic)

PALENQUE
The Palace (Late Classic)

CHIAPAS

YAXCHILÁN
Detail from a lintel
(Late Classic)

Sierra

SEIBAL
Limestone stela
(Late Classic)

GUATEMALA

Madre

QUIRIGUÁ
Sandstone stela
(Late Classic)

HICHÉN ITZÁ
  Nunnery Quadrangle (Post-Classic)

ISLAND OF COZUMEL

TULUM
The Castillo
(Late Post-Classic)

LIZE

Gulf of Honduras

)PÁN
  Acropolis (Late Clàssic)

HONDURAS

At the time of the Spanish Conquest the area occupied by peoples speaking the Maya languages stretched from the Yucatán peninsula to the Pacific coast of Guatemala and from the coastal plains of Tabasco to the areas of Honduras and El Salvador adjoining Guatemala. The civilization of the Classic period, from the 4th to the 10th century, spread first into the central lowlands, then up into the Yucatán. The Post-Classic civilizations mainly occupied the north of the peninsula. The precocious development in the highlands in the Pre-Classic period was not matched by similar achievements in the lowlands.

I n August 1839 the invention of the daguerreotype raised high hopes in the intellectual world. The development of photography led to a generation of photographer-explorers who set out on the quest for "objective" truth.

CHAPTER IV
THE PHOTOGRAPHER-
EXPLORERS

"Yucatán is without question the area that is richest in ruined American monuments. It is covered with them from north to south, and we will find there the largest, the most important, and the most wonderful creations of these native civilizations."
Désiré Charnay
Un Voyage au Yucatán
1863

During the second half of the 19th century Western scholars became convinced that the ruins of Chiapas, the Petén, and the Yucatán derived from a single civilization that owed nothing to the Greeks, Egyptians, or Hindus. From then on, Maya civilization took on a new significance and a new value in their eyes. The sheer extent of its territory, the length of time it seemed to have lasted, the splendor of its art and architecture, and the fascinating complexities of its script established it firmly alongside the great civilizations of the West.

The Maya ruins were no longer thought of as simply a picturesque background for painters or an ideal spot to inspire dreamers and poets. Once they had been recognized as the remains of a long-lost, civilized nation, they became the subject of academic scrutiny. And at the time, the Maya nation seemed superior even to that of the Aztecs, who

were still considered barbarians because of their practice of human sacrifice—in contrast, it was then thought, to the Maya.

The task facing scholars was to study Maya civilization with all the serious attention and scientific objectivity it deserved. It was the development of photography that helped to make this possible. On their second trip Stephens and Catherwood had taken with them equipment for making daguerreotypes, experimenting by taking pictures first of themselves, then of the young beauties in Mérida, and finally of the ruins of Uxmal. In spite of some initial success, the deteriorating quality of their results eventually led them to abandon the technique.

"Torn by brambles and our bodies covered in garrapatas [ticks]…, we arrived at the Nunnery Palace, the most important of the monuments in Chichén Itzá…. I set up my things in one of the rooms… and the Indians set to work."
Désiré Charnay
Un Voyage au Yucatán
1863

Photography Was Still in Its Infancy, and the Explorers Had to Carry Several Hundred Pounds of Equipment

It is to the Frenchman Désiré Charnay that credit must go for taking and publishing the first photographs of the Maya ruins. He must have developed a taste for travel quite early on, as it was while teaching in New Orleans that he discovered his true vocation through reading Stephens. He made up his mind to explore the ruins of the ancient Mexicans and of the Maya and to fix their image forever on photosensitive plates. He traveled back across the Atlantic, waited patiently for appointments in the various French

Charnay obtained excellent results, despite having to use collodion negatives. The collodion dried rapidly, which meant that each glass plate had to be prepared just before the picture was taken and developed immediately afterwards. The photographs above show the Castillo at Chichén Itzá (top) and the Nunnery Quadrangle in Uxmal (also at left).

ministries, and in 1857 finally succeeded in obtaining a grant from the Ministry for State Education. He set sail for Veracruz, via the United States, in November of that year. In September 1858 he left Mexico City for Oaxaca with 4000 pounds of luggage. The cumbersome equipment made traveling very difficult; apart from the camera itself, with its tripod, there was a whole assortment of chemicals and glass plates, which had to be carefully packaged if they were to survive several days of being jolted on the back of a mule. Charnay discovered en route that the country was unsafe and, not wishing to risk losing his precious equipment, he resolved to entrust it to the mule drivers, who would take a longer but safer route.

He waited more than five months in Oaxaca for his luggage to arrive. Frustrated by his enforced inactivity, he decided, improvising with local materials, to embark on a series of photographs taken in Mitla, a mountainous region where villages had sprung up in narrow river valleys separated by lofty, snow-covered mountains. It was to be the source of many disappointments and problems, which led him to the verge of despair. But in spite of the appalling conditions, Charnay managed to produce a series of photographs for *Cités et ruines américaines* (*American Cities and Ruins*), a large and expensive volume containing forty-seven original prints and two photolithographs of Mitla, Palenque, Izamal,

On his second expedition to Mexico Charnay (left), now more experienced and with less restrictive photographic techniques at his disposal, tackled new subjects. In Mérida he set up his tripod in the market (below). And on the high plateau of central Mexico he captured an Indian in the act of sucking the sap *(aguamiel)* from an agave with the aid of a long gourd (right). Its contents would then be poured into the wineskin carried on his back and fermented to produce *pulque*, the traditional drink of the highland Mexicans.

Chichén Itzá, and Uxmal. Although this work, which appeared in 1863, was not widely distributed, it was favorably received by the critics.

The Camera Recorded the Elegant Proportions of the Buildings—But Also the Ravages of Time

The most successful views, taken mainly in Chichén Itzá and Uxmal, reveal both the impressive monumentality of the buildings and the richness of their decoration. Yet they also convey a depressing picture of decay. Facades have been cracked apart, walls have collapsed into piles of rubble, while the original shape of the elaborate temples, set as if by a

Charnay conformed to the fashion among contemporary travelers for photographing men and women as physical specimens. Like all these images, the "Maya types," shown full face and in profile, were published in the form of engravings based on Charnay's photographs.

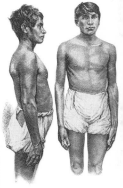

divine hand on top of hills covered with undergrowth and debris, can scarcely be imagined. Nature is ever-present; the foregrounds of the photographs are often obscured by a tangle of trees and bushes, though there are signs that these have been largely hacked away for the purposes of the shot. In spite of the care taken by

This small, Puuc-style temple, nicknamed la Iglesia, the church, was photographed by Charnay in 1860.

the photographer and his assistants to clear them away, trees spring miraculously from piles of stone, lianas crisscross the facades, and bushes sprout thickly on the tops of the temples.

Charnay made photographic expeditions to Madagascar, Java, and Australia before returning to Mexico in 1864, this time with the troops of the force sent to support the Emperor Maximilian. He then traveled to the United States and South America.

Finally, in 1880, over twenty years after his first visit, he returned to Mexico, where he continued his work, both as a photographer and as an archaeologist. From March to November Charnay carried out excavations in central Mexico, mainly in Tula and Teotihuacán. He visited Comalcalco, the westernmost Maya city, and in pouring rain he cleared the undergrowth and measured the ruined buildings, taking photographs whenever there was a break in the clouds. He spent five difficult weeks in Palenque. The workmen he had employed to clear the trees worked too slowly for his liking or deserted him altogether, and the rain fell almost every day, hampering every kind of operation and distorting the camera until it was quite unusable.

Prompted by the Same Concern for Objectivity That Made Him Take Up Photography, Charnay Made Papier-Mâché Casts

He laid up to six layers of wet newspaper over the bas-reliefs and then left them to dry in the open air or by the fire. This was a risky business, however; on the night of 26 January 1880 every one of his casts caught fire, and he had to spend ten days working nonstop to rebuild his collection. These casts, which provide

Charnay made casts of sculptures of various shapes and sizes, including a trapezoid of two-headed celestial serpents of increasing length (top) and the statue of a *chacmool*, or offering carrier (above); the reclining male figure holds in his lap a circular dish where offerings were placed. Such *chacmool* figures can be found in Chichén Itzá and in Tula (Hidalgo, Mexico) about 1200 miles away.

accurate, three-dimensional copies of the original sculptures, are today in the Musée de l'Homme in Paris. In contrast to the views taken in 1858–60, this time Charnay's photographs were not intended to appear as an album of original prints but were reproduced as engravings to illustrate articles and books. The best known of these was his *Anciennes villes du nouveau monde (Ancient Cities of the New World)*, published in 1885. What they lost in grandeur, they made up for in naturalness, for Charnay was now quite happy to photograph a forest encampment, a collection of objects found in the course of his excavations, or his rough and ready living conditions in the Palace of Palenque. The photographer seems more at ease with his subject matter, and his views are less stilted, less "official" than before.

After Palenque Charnay visited sites in the Yucatán (Izamal, Chichén Itzá, Kabah, Uxmal) and then embarked on a long and difficult trek, lasting nearly two weeks, towards some ruins he had heard about. He was eager to gain the credit for being the "discoverer" of the site that is known today as Yaxchilán. Only a few hours short of the ruins, however, he learned that another explorer was already there; one can imagine his disappointment and annoyance. He sent his card to the stranger, and the next day the two men met.

Charnay could tell at once that his rival, who was twenty-two years his junior, was an Englishman, "a man of the world, and a gentleman." He introduced himself as Alfred Maudslay of St. James's Club, Piccadilly, London. Sensing the French scholar's irritation, Maudslay went to great lengths to salve his pride: "I am only an amateur, traveling for the fun of it; you are an expert, and the city belongs to you." Charnay magnanimously assured his fellow explorer that they would share the credit for discovering "Lorillard City," as he called it, in honor of his patron.

As we can see from these photographs of the Maudslays taken during their trip to Guatemala in 1894, the mule was—until about 1950—the method of transport most frequently used by archaeologists. In spite of its drawbacks, Charnay may have thought it was infinitely preferable to being carried in a chair on an Indian's back… especially during a tropical rainstorm, when one would be soaked to the skin (right).

It Is Impossible to Imagine Two More Incompatible Characters Than the Loquacious Latin Charnay and the Reserved Anglo-Saxon Maudslay

Maudslay confided his true opinion of the Frenchman to his journal: "He does not strike me as a scientific traveler of much class—he is a pleasant, talkative gentleman, thirsting for glory." Charnay dreamed of grand theories that would bring him lasting fame: "[He] burst on me in the first few minutes of our acquaintance with the fact that he has established a great theory about the ruined cities…which means that he had set to work to upset the utterly unnecessary theory that the cities are of great antiquity." Nevertheless, the men managed to live and work together, on good terms, for several days, and Charnay taught Maudslay his technique for making papier-mâché casts.

It was Maudslay's second trip to Central America, but his first with a particular aim in mind. Two years before, inspired by his reading of Stephens, he had traveled to Guatemala as a tourist to visit Quiriguá, Copán, and Tikal. He later explained how, while clearing moss from a monument in Quiriguá, "As the curious outlines of the carved ornament gathered shape it began to dawn upon me how much more important were these monuments, upon which I had stumbled almost by chance, than any account I had heard of them had led me to expect. This day's work induced me to take a permanent interest in Central American archaeology, and a journey which was undertaken merely to escape the rigors of an English winter has been followed by seven expeditions from England for the purpose of further exploration and archaeological research."

Maudslay abandoned his career as a colonial administrator, which had taken him first to Trinidad,

When Maudslay returned to Quiriguá in 1883 (the camp is shown opposite) he was accompanied by an expert in cast-making, who had come specially from London. The specialist's main task was to create a cast of the monument known unofficially as the Great Turtle.

The finished cast was made up of over 600 separate elements, requiring nearly 2 tons of plaster. The huge sandstone rock, 7 feet high and 10 feet long, and covered with carvings, is an image of the two-headed earth monster.

then to Queensland, Australia, and finally to Fiji. Three important factors helped him in his new enterprise: he was used to the tropical climate and terrain, he had a great interest in the native languages and cultures of the countries in which he stayed, and he was an excellent photographer. Born in 1850 into a family of industrialists, he had private means, and though he was not especially rich, he had no need to work for a living.

Suspicious of Over-Hasty Interpretations, Maudslay Trusted Only Reliable Evidence

Unmoved by Charnay's elaborate theories, the more methodical Maudslay remained convinced that to find out more about this lost civilization, they first had to investigate the surviving remains. There was, of course, all the information that lay buried underground, awaiting the picks and spades of the excavators, but there was also the visible world of the Maya—their buildings and sculptures—which Stephens, Catherwood, and then Charnay had started to record. To improve their understanding of the civilization, they would have to have access to completely reliable documentation—the architecture, carved images, and hieroglyphic texts would have to be reproduced as accurately as possible.

Maudslay used three techniques to achieve this: photography, casting, and drawing. By 1882 he had an extra advantage over Charnay; the dry gelatin negative had just been invented. The glass plates could now be prepared in advance and did not have to be developed

From this model plan of the center of Copán (above), by Anne Hunter, we can gauge the extent of the damage caused to the ruins by the river, which continued to wear away at the site until 1936, when the Carnegie Institution diverted its course.

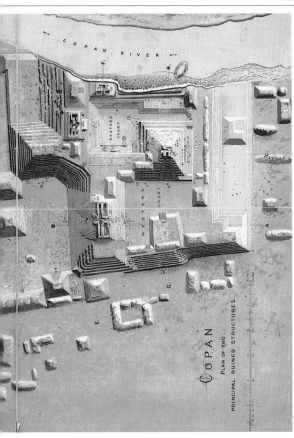

When he entered the Temple of the Jaguars in Chichén Itzá in 1888, Maudslay did not expect to find much trace of the paintings discovered by Stephens forty-five years earlier. But in spite of some damage caused by damp and the local villagers, he was able to copy several scenes: a human sacrifice, a battle, and a somewhat unexpected landscape scene showing a village at the edge of a forest full of animals, which is reminiscent of works by the early 20th-century French primitivist painter Henri Rousseau.

immediately after they had been exposed. This enormous step forward lightened the luggage of the photographer-explorers considerably and saved them a great deal of trouble. Maudslay also perfected Charnay's casting technique; using an outer layer of plaster to produce more precise, less flimsy casts, he was able to make copies of carvings in high relief, such as the stelae from Copán. This work proved costly, however, in terms of both patience and transport; for just one season's work (three months) in Copán, for example, Maudslay used 4 tons of plaster and 600 pounds of paper. Convoys of local Maya must then have been required to carry the casts several days' journey to Izamal, on the Río Dulce, where they would have been loaded onto a ship. At New Orleans they were transferred to another vessel bound for England. Maudslay's casts, which produced near-perfect copies of the originals, were immensely popular in exhibitions and museums.

Maler Fell in Love with Mexico

Teobert Maler, the last of the great explorers, was born in Rome in 1842, of German parents. He studied engineering and architecture in Karlsruhe before moving to Vienna, where he acquired Austrian citizenship. When the Emperor Maximilian gained the Mexican throne he joined the volunteer force of the Mexican imperial army, and for the eighteen months leading up to the emperor's execution in 1867 he was involved in every major battle. Returning to civilian life, he traveled across the country taking photographs, on both plates and film, first of the villages, then of the ruins. Like everyone else, he began with Mitla, which was both accessible and photogenic, before moving on, predictably, to Palenque, which he visited three times in 1877. The following year he returned to Europe to begin long-drawn-out legal proceedings in support of his claim to a family inheritance. His knowledge of Mexico and its history, combined with the fine quality of his photographs, meant that French Americanists happily opened their doors to him. He took advantage of his stay to write articles, give lectures (to the Société de Géographie, for instance—complete with slides!), and to read all he could about the Maya.

In 1884 Maler returned to Mexico, having won his court case and a small fortune, which he was to devote to his exploration of the Maya ruins. Having established himself in Ticul, a small Yucatecan town, he visited and photographed several sites, many of which

In 1913 Teobert Maler (above) took several remarkable photographs. The one shown at right provides an excellent illustration of the steeply sloping vaults found in Palenque. The external slope of the roof, which was parallel to that of the internal vault, allowed the builders to construct larger interior spaces and to introduce numerous openings into the walls. Nevertheless, the Maya corbel had no keystone, so to create these interior spaces the Maya built two walls that grew increasingly thicker until they met at the top. The resulting space captured the qualities of the domestic hut.

Palenque

he was the first to record in this way. In 1895, along with a few Indians to clear the vegetation, Maler traveled as far as the ruins of the Petén and the Usumacinta River. Whenever he reached a new site, he would look for the best angle and, if necessary, have a platform built for his camera. He would wait patiently for the wind to drop or the cloud to lift before pressing the switch that worked the shutter. He would always develop the photographs before leaving the site, and would not hesitate to retake any shots he was not completely satisfied with.

In 1898 the Peabody Museum, Harvard University, asked him to undertake a series of expeditions in Maya country; proper reports were published on his explorations, with itineraries, descriptions, plans, sketches, and of course his famous photographs. Many smaller

In Uxmal one of the groups of buildings is known as the Cemetery, because the sides of a platform discovered there were decorated with bas-reliefs showing skulls and crossbones. Far from representing dead citizens who had been piously buried by the community, these skulls stand for victims who were sacrificed to the gods.

sites, as well as a few more important ones in Chiapas, the Usumacinta valley, and in the Petén (such as Piedras Negras and Naranjo) were documented for the first time. In 1905 he argued with his employers, who then appointed someone else to lead a fourth Maya expedition. An embittered Maler found it hard to resign himself to this enforced retirement; after two years in Europe he returned to Mexico, dying in Mérida in 1907.

Until 1891 Most Explorers and Archaeologists Were Happy to Study the Visible Remains

Maler made no attempt to excavate the many sites he visited. It was the Peabody Museum that first organized teams of people to carry out scientific excavations in Copán, between 1891 and 1895. They produced a plan of the center of the site, cleared plazas and buildings, drew up an inventory of the monuments, investigated the offerings associated with them, and excavated some tombs.

Yet these digs revealed very little about the Maya. Still almost nothing was known about the full extent of the sites, about their age or how long they had been occupied. The archaeologists remained silent on the function of the buildings and knew little about the objects created there, whether of pottery, jade, or bone. How could they begin to describe Maya funerary customs, for example, when so few tombs had been investigated?

On the other hand, hundreds of stone monuments had been photographed or drawn; three codices had been published, as well as several of the major chronicles on the Maya and their history. The raw material was there. Thousands of glyphs and hundreds of carved and painted images were just waiting to be interpreted.

Contrary to what one might expect from this section of a temple drawn by Maler, the Maya pyramids are solid, although sometimes perforated by interior burial chambers, as at Palenque. On the left can be seen the outline of the steps, or blocks of decreasing size placed one above the other, while on the right is the central staircase. The whole pyramid acted as the base for a relatively small temple.

E very visitor to Palenque who sees the hieroglyph-covered panels in the Temple of Inscriptions experiences the same emotions that overwhelmed Stephens: "The impression made upon our minds by these speaking but unintelligible tablets I shall not attempt to describe."

CHAPTER V

SYMBOLS IN STONE

With a total height of 39 feet, stela E in Quiriguá, erected in 771, is the largest known Maya sculpture (left). On the front and back is carved a full-length portrait of a king, while the sides bear a long inscription. The disk on the right shows a Chinkultik ballplayer preparing to strike a ball.

Before Catherwood, few artists had tried to copy the glyphs on the Maya temples and sculptures. Del Río's report was illustrated with two plates of inscriptions, each showing six hieroglyphs, while Galindo gave only a few examples. In each case they did not intend to produce accurate copies—in fact, the drawings are very hard to make out at all—but simply to give an impression of what the Maya characters looked like. Clearly, the explorers and their artists were discouraged; what was the point of copying texts no one could understand, and, they assumed, never would? Stephens must have had more faith in the future and in scientific progress, but he too was forced to admit that the texts were "unintelligible."

Waldeck often had difficulty in reproducing the Maya glyphs. This text, from the Temple of the Inscriptions, was at the time covered with bird and bat droppings, so he completed any illegible glyphs with his own additions, such as cuneiform signs and elephant heads.

In 1866 Brasseur de Bourbourg Claimed "The Key to These Hieroglyphs Has Today Been Found; All That Remains Is to Find How to Make Use of It"

The story of how the Maya script was deciphered begins with Brasseur's publication in 1864 of Landa's *Relación de las Cosas de Yucatán*. Landa first explains the calendar cycle of eighteen periods *(uinal)* of twenty days *(kin)* each, or 360 days, to which were added five unlucky days *(uayeyab)*, bringing the total

It was realized quite early on that Landa's alphabet (above) did not include the vast majority of Maya characters and so could not be used to explain everything.

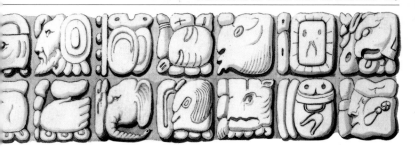

to 365. "For these 360 days they have twenty letters or characters, by which they name them, omitting to give a name to the other five days, since they considered them unlucky and bad." The chronicler drew each character with its name underneath: *Kan, Chicchan, Cimi, Manik,* etc. Landa also described the festivities and ceremonies associated with each month, again giving the name and the glyph for each one: *Pop, Uo, Zotz, Tzec,* etc.

Landa wanted to understand the "alphabet" used by these people, but as he could only conceive of an alphabetical system of writing, there began a veritable dialogue of the deaf between the bishop and his informant, an educated Maya nobleman. Landa chose as his examples Maya words of one syllable, but which were written in Spanish with two letters. For example, the Maya word for water, *ha,* is written with "h" (pronounced "a-tché" in Spanish) and "a." The Maya nobleman therefore wrote down the characters that were closest to what the Spanish bishop wanted: one sign for "a," another for "tché," and a third for "a."

At the time of the Conquest, the Maya calculated the date using *katuns* (20 years of 360 days), each one being represented by its last day, or *ahau,* preceded by a number. In this method there were thirteen *katuns,* with a fixed *katun* (4 *ahau,* for example) recurring after 256 years. This cycle, which is called the *katun* round, can be illustrated by a form of wheel turning counterclockwise (left). The black cross at the top of the drawing acts as a reference point.

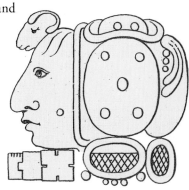

He was in fact writing the sounds of the Spanish letters, exactly as if, in English, he had written "wagon": "double-you-ay-gee-o-en."

The complete lack of understanding between the two men increased still further when, towards the end of the session, Landa asked his informant to write down any sentence; the Indian, exasperated by the absurdity of the whole exercise, wrote: *ma in kati* (I don't want to!).

Obsessed with Deciphering the Calendar, the Researchers Forgot That the Dates Must Be Dating Something!

The reason why the first "decoders" spent so much time puzzling over the numbers and the calendar was that their work was based on the information supplied by Landa. Some, including Brasseur de Bourbourg and Léon de Rosny, tried to apply his notorious "alphabet," but with no success. Others, such as Ernst Förstemann and J. T. Goodman, began by comparing the inscriptions in the codices and on the monuments, and identifying the glyphs for the days and months. Starting from these calendrical elements, they managed to decipher others, and eventually worked out how the different dating cycles were used. They were assisted in their task by the relative importance of the calendar in the inscriptions. Almost half of the symbols on the Panel of the Ninety-Six Glyphs in Palenque, for example, are calendrical, and this is by no means unusual.

Naturally, the researchers tended to stress the parts of the inscriptions that they were beginning, through painstaking research, to understand, at the expense of those that remained stubbornly "unintelligible," As they discovered fairly early on that the Maya erected their carved stelae at regular intervals (usually every five years), they began to speak of a "stela cult." They characterized the Maya as time worshipers, and wrongly labeled as "gods" any anthropomorphic glyphs relating to periods or numbers.

On this stela from Quiriguá the upper half of the inscription is composed of full-figure, animated hieroglyphs, which here take the place of the more usual grotesque heads and other characters.

The seventy-fourth page of the *Dresden Codex* shows the world being destroyed by flood, or perhaps, more prosaically, the onset of the rainy season. The celestial monster has the head of a caiman and the feet of a deer, and its body is covered with celestial signs: Venus, sun, sky, darkness. Torrential rain pours from the monster's mouth, while additional floods descend from symbols for the sun and moon. An aged goddess is also making rain by emptying an earthenware jar over the world. At the bottom of the image crouches god L, one of the rulers of the Underworld. He is armed with spears and a long staff, and on his head he carries the moan bird, his emblem.

The Texts Rarely Appear in Isolation; Both in the Codices and on the Monuments, They Are Associated with Images

One might expect the decoding of the glyphs to facilitate a correct interpretation of the images, and vice versa…assuming, that is, there is a link between text and image, the former commenting on the latter, and the image illustrating the inscription. And one might expect still more to emerge from a clear understanding of the images: information about the Maya people, their customs, and beliefs.

Before the images could be interpreted, however, it was first necessary to "see" the image clearly, that is, to recognize and identify the individual motifs from which it was composed. In other words, before the significance of the serpent could be determined, the serpent had first to be recognized as such within the image. And this was often no easy matter, even for the specialist. Maya art makes no attempt to be realistic; it expresses not

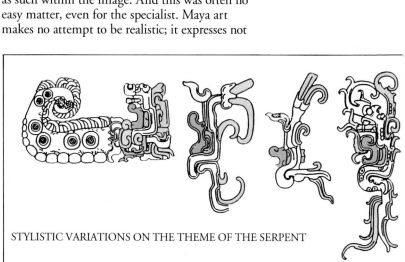

STYLISTIC VARIATIONS ON THE THEME OF THE SERPENT

what is seen, but what is known. The true appearance of the subject is modified until it is almost completely unrecognizable when compared with the original. Maya artists altered the proportions, placed glyphs over the eyes, stripped jawbones down to the bare bones beneath, gave serpents large jade earflares, and drew bird wings like the jaws of a reptile.

Decoding was further complicated by the sheer accumulation and interweaving of the motifs that made up the image. Some Maya reliefs look, at first sight, like a bowl of spaghetti; tangled forms cover every inch, leaving not the slightest blank space. The eye gets lost and can make out nothing. The phrase "horror of the void" has been used in connection with the technique, but it derives rather from a desire to express as much as possible in the space available, with no hesitation about repeating the same "message" several times over, usually in different forms.

Little by Little Common Motifs Were Distinguished—Among Them the Famous Serpent

The first explorers and the artists who accompanied them admitted that they had difficulty in understanding the images they discovered. Their work betrays this difficulty; in Castañeda's drawing of a mask from Palenque, which decorates the pedestal for a figure, for instance, although he has copied all the separate elements (eyes, muzzle, etc.), it is clear that he sees them only as unconnected shapes, and not as a mask.

Maudslay was the first person truly to "understand" the images. Even better, he used colored drawings to help his readers isolate the individual motifs. He also pointed to the recurrence of certain themes by collecting examples from various sites.

The serpent is the most common natural form in Maya art. A human or mythical head is often shown emerging from its open mouth. This was the Maya way of representing the appearance in this world of a creature belonging to the other world. Simplified serpent heads express sacred power.

He provided evidence of the use made in Maya art of the "feathered serpent," the "head and scroll of the feathered serpent," of "grotesque faces," and of the "serpent-bird."

Herbert J. Spinden and Tatiana Proskouriakoff continued Maudslay's study of Maya art, especially in its most spectacular form: sculpture. But style was still more important to them than the meaning of the images. Who were these men, and occasionally women, carved on the stelae, panels, and lintels? Were they kings, priests, or gods? Who were the figures, who

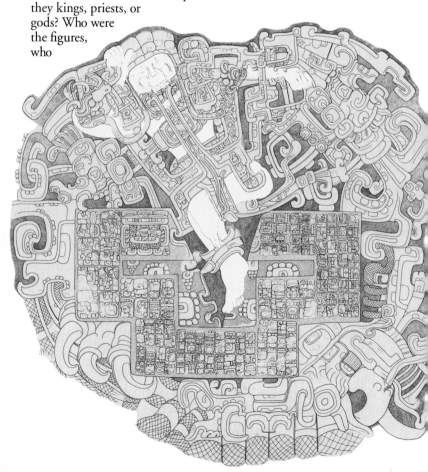

seemed to be of lesser rank, standing by their sides? Were they acolytes, members of their family, or perhaps the rulers of other cities? And what of the half-naked figures crouching at the feet of the main figure? Were they slaves, captives, or sacrificial victims? What could be the significance of the grimacing masks, the mythical, reptilian, and feline creatures, or the headdresses and ceremonial robes, writhing with heads, symbolic objects, and feathers?

Without the help of writing, which could at that time only provide help with dates, it was extremely difficult to interpret these images. The codices, on the other hand, allowed various gods to be identified, as the glyphs that stood for them were often to be found in the inscription above the image. In this way, for example, a close parallel was demonstrated between the drawings on pages 25 to 28 of the *Dresden Codex* and Landa's description of the new year's festivities; it became clear that they must refer to the same ceremonies.

In the first half of the 20th century, by studying the development of architecture, sculpture, and pottery, and using the dates on the monuments to help them, archaeologists divided Maya history into four main periods: Pre-Classic (1500 B.C.–A.D. 300), Early Classic (300–600), Late Classic (600–900) and Post-Classic (900–1527), each period subdivided into early and late phases. This is the chronological framework still in use today.

In the drawing of an altar from Quiriguá (opposite, below), the king, who has just died, is wearing a jaguar mask symbolizing the night sun, with which the king is identified. He brandishes a two-headed snake, which here stands for death and sacrifice, as he descends into the Underworld through a V-shaped crack in the earth, conventionally shown as a broad letter T, which carries the monument's inscription. Above the drawing is the calendrical notation *O kin* from the Palace Tablet at Palenque.

In his study of stela B in Copán (left), Maudslay used watercolors to help his readers distinguish the different parts of the drawing. The coloring highlights the muzzle of the earth monster above the king's head, flanked by two macaw heads; the two serpent heads decorating each end of the scepter the king carries in his arms; and the masks and bells hanging from his waist.

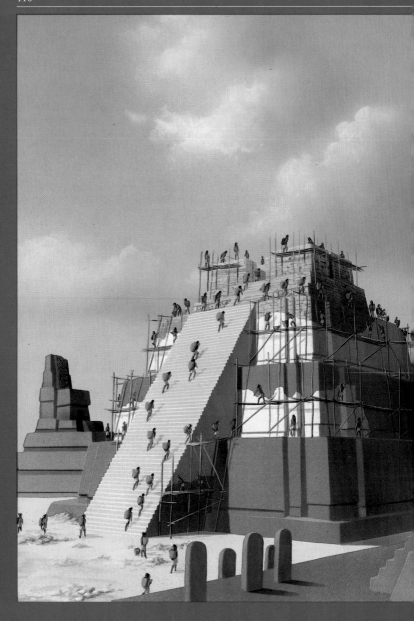

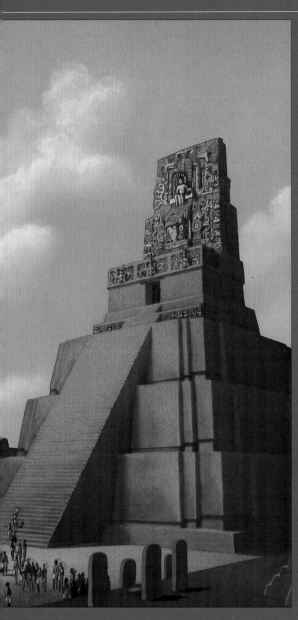

Building a Pyramid

About 130 feet high, Temple II in Tikal stands on the main plaza, opposite Temple I. Dating from the very early 8th century, it is built on a terraced pyramid made up of three platforms of decreasing size. These are made of solid rubble contained by outer walls, which are covered with a thick layer of stucco, carefully smoothed, then painted red. The temple itself, made up of three narrow rooms, was constructed on a tall, narrow platform at the summit of the pyramid and was surmounted by a hollow roof comb twice the height of the temple itself. A single carved wooden lintel still survives from this temple; it depicts a noblewoman (maybe the wife of the king known as ruler A), whose remains are entombed under the pyramid of Temple I.

The Oldest Known Maya Construction

This pyramid in Uaxactún, about 16 miles northwest of Tikal, was erected at the beginning of our modern era, that is, long before the great achievements of the Classic period. It supported a temple built of perishable materials, and its four huge stairways were flanked by eighteen vast serpent and jaguar masks made of stucco, illustrating the fundamental opposition of the Maya cosmology. This is the earliest known example of a pyramid with four staircases, the plan of which no doubt represents the division of the cosmos into four quadrants. Although today the structure is brilliant white, it is likely that, along with the majority of the pyramids that came after it, it was once daubed with blood-red paint.

A Political and Ceremonial Center

The center of Copán, as it may have looked towards the end of the 8th century, at the time of its greatest splendor. On the left (that is, to the north) lies the main square, or plaza, where the rituals and processions probably took place; it is surrounded by stairways, which may have acted as seating for the onlookers. It was here that most of the site's stelae and altars were found. The ball court near the center of the picture is flanked on its east and west sides by two parallel buildings, and on the northern edge by an L-shaped platform. On the right, the acropolis includes various buildings grouped around two courts. Thanks to their architectural character- istics and the themes treated in the sculpted decoration, it has been possible to establish the function of some of these buildings: a royal residence, a temple dedicated to the founder of the ruling dynasty, and another temple built over a royal tomb. It has also been possible to identify the buildings that acted as stages for the perfor- mance of religious rituals.

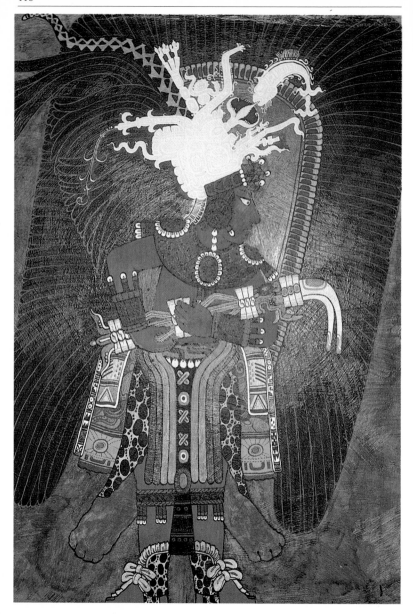

117

In 1944 the photographer Giles Healey set out for a remote corner of the Chiapas jungle. The powerful United Fruit Company had asked him to make a film about the Lacandon Indians, a Maya tribe who, living in this region, had managed to preserve their ancient traditions intact. Few explorers had ventured that far.

CHAPTER VI
FROM IMAGE TO REALITY

The murals of Bonampak illustrate scenes from royal life between 790 and 792. The first room shows the presentation of an heir and the celebration of his acceptance by the court. Here (left) we see the reigning Bonampak king, Chaan-muan, in full regalia, from his jaguar sandals and feather backframe to the boa constrictor in his headdress.

The Lacandon Indians treated the ruins of their ancestors with great respect, believing them to be the dwelling places of their gods, and they went there regularly to make offerings, burn incense, and pray. They usually refused to take white people to see these *tuns*, or "stones," as they called their sacred sites. Nevertheless, in the case of Giles Healey they made an exception, because he had brought them some of the "benefits" of civilization: hunting rifles and ammunition, clothes, food, and medicine.

With the help of his Lacandon friends, Healey had already discovered about twenty sites in the region, most of them of minor importance, when in May 1946 one of his hunting companions, José Pepe Chan Bor, led him to a larger group of ruins. He explored and photographed the temples, perched high up on the summit of ruined pyramids, and came across impressive carved stelae. He then found his way into one of the largest buildings on the site, which had three entrances.

Unable to see anything in the darkened interior, Healey went out again, made a torch, then reentered. After a few seconds, once his eyes had become accustomed to the gloom, he gazed around him, awestruck; on the walls and vault of the small room were painted several multicolored figures. Entering by the second doorway, he found himself in an identical room decorated with many more reclining and standing figures. It was the same with the third and final room.

This discovery, at a site soon named Bonampak by the scholar Sylvanus G. Morley, was of major importance. No one had suspected the high quality of Maya painting, as virtually all examples had disappeared; these, however, were exceptionally well preserved.

There is as yet no satisfactory record of the complete set of murals in Bonampak. The painting on the left is a detail from the original.

The north wall of the second room, from a 1948 reconstruction (below), shows the king and his court reviewing the naked captives, many of whom have had their fingernails pulled out, prior to sacrifice.

At First Even the Top Specialists Refused to Recognize What the Frescoes of Bonampak Reveal

In 1947 and 1948 the Carnegie Institution of Washington and the National Institute of Anthropology and History in Mexico sent experts to study the paintings firsthand and artists to make copies of them. The first important study to be published in English appeared in 1955, but it failed to question any of the traditionally accepted theories about the Maya. The more aggressive aspects of the paintings—there were scenes of torture and

A t the foot of the steps the warriors stand guard. At the top of the pyramid more richly dressed nobles surround the king. The frieze above them, which represents the sky, includes the symbols for certain constellations.

decapitation—were minimized, and the political implications of the court scenes avoided. Scholars such as Morley, for example, persisted in clinging to their original hypotheses, but the pictures spoke for themselves; as the violence of some of the scenes began to be noted, the image of the Maya as a peace-loving people grew less and less convincing. The word "theocracy" began to provoke wry smiles, and the omnipotence of the "calendar priests" was questioned. Nevertheless, it was some time before scholars noticed that the same individuals reappeared in several scenes and before they could identify them, thanks to the accompanying inscriptions. In other words, the historical nature of the paintings was the most difficult aspect to accept.

In 1949 Mexican Archaeologists Took Center Stage as Systematic Excavations Began in Palenque

Under the direction of Alberto Ruz Lhuillier the first of ten seasons of excavations began. Ruz wanted to investigate the Temple of Inscriptions, the most majestic of them all, in the hope of discovering whether it stood on the remains of a more ancient, pre-Maya structure. No excavations had been attempted on this site since Maudslay's day.

First, the pyramid and its surroundings were cleared of undergrowth, together with the temple interior, where three panels carried one of the longest known Maya inscriptions, composed of some 617 glyphs. In the middle room Ruz noticed that one of the stone floor slabs had a double row of holes, through which ropes could be passed to move it. Nearby another slab lay broken as the result of an unofficial dig, perhaps the responsibility of del Río. Ruz then noticed that the temple wall did not stop at ground level, but continued below it; intrigued by this, he began to dig at this spot, and 31 inches down he found a stone that seemed to have been laid as part

In the crypt at Palenque several life-size stucco models of human heads were found. They may have come from the medallions that decorate the walls of building A of the Palace, rather in the manner of a gallery of ancestors in a European stately home. If these medallions do in fact represent historical figures, these heads would be portraits of the dead king or his ancestors.

The sarcophagus lid shows the dead King Pacal atop the setting sun as he falls into the gaping, skeletal jaws of the earth monster. From the center of the king's body grows the World Tree, the Maya *axis mundi*, topped by a great celestial bird. In death the king has taken on the characteristics of two gods, one of which is the maize god, a symbol of annual renewal.

of a vault. He dug through it, and 7 feet further down he uncovered a step, followed by a second, then a third. His curiosity had led him into a vaulted stairway completely filled with rubble, which, he calculated, led westward into the pyramid. The next year he followed the steps down to a depth of 50 feet, where he reached a landing. Here the stairs turned at a right angle towards the north, then east, before descending further.

During the third season thirteen more steps were uncovered, and by the beginning of the fourth season—it was now 1952—Ruz knew he could not be far from the end, because he was now beneath the level of the foot of the pyramid. Cutting his way through a roughly built wall of rocks and clay, he came to another wall, 6 feet further on, more carefully constructed of stone. Between the two was a small box containing offerings: pottery, shells, cinnabar (powdered mercury), and jade. The staircase was replaced by a corridor.

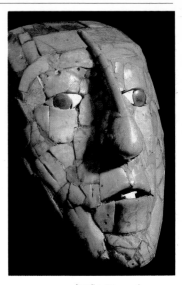

This Maya ruler was buried with his face covered by a death mask made completely of jade, apart from the eyes and teeth. The figurine with a mythical face (above right) and the mask representing the sun god (right) are also made of this semi-precious stone. The sun mask is characterized by its crossed eyes, and Landa says that for this reason Maya mothers tried to make their children squint by dangling a bead of pitch between their eyes.

Year by Year, Step by Step, Ruz Was Working His Way Towards a Truly Overwhelming Discovery

The second wall hid a tightly packed layer of rocks and lime 13 feet thick. Crossing this, the excavators found two more steps leading onto another landing, where there was a second casket—this time containing the remains of six human sacrificial victims. The end of the corridor was blocked from top to bottom by a vast triangular slab.

Using a crowbar, one of the workmen smashed a small gap filled with lime and pebbles. Ruz knelt down, pressed his eye to the opening, a light in one hand, and remained there in silence, without moving a muscle. His companions, becoming increasingly impatient, began to press him with questions. Eventually, he rose and, with great emotion, described a large vaulted room, its walls decorated with stucco reliefs; in the center of the room, filling it almost completely, was a vast carved block of stone. Removing the slab that sealed this crypt, they

descended the four steps that led into it. The large block, the sides of which were carved with ten figures, rested on six supports, also ornamented with carvings. It was covered by a stone slab measuring 13 x 7 feet, decorated all over with bas-reliefs; in the foreground of a vast composition representing the cosmos, a man—the dead—was shown falling into the open jaws of the earth monster. An inscription ran around the edges of the slab.

For the Maya jade was a symbol of life and immortality. There is hardly any tomb or offering that does not contain at least a fragment of jade.

Ruz picked up the offerings that lay on the surface of the slab before it was levered off (using some truck jacks) to reveal a sarcophagus, the top of which was pierced by a bottle-shaped cavity sealed by a cover.

When this was lifted, they found beneath it the skeleton of a man, his face covered by a jade mosaic death mask, with eyes of shell and obsidian. The skeleton was covered with jewelry: pendants, a diadem, ear ornaments, necklace, pectoral, bracelets, and rings, all made of the purest jade, the Maya's most precious material.

Stunned and thrilled by the discovery of this treasure, fascinated by the technical achievement represented by the pyramid, and astonished by the beauty of the offerings and sculptures, the scholarly world and the general public were also profoundly shocked. Did this mean that the Maya pyramids had played some funerary role, just like those of ancient Egypt? Even Ruz himself refused to accept the full implications of his discovery, preferring to consider Palenque an exceptional case. Soon, however, the discovery of other royal tombs—notably in Tikal—confirmed the new hypothesis.

After Bonampak and the Tomb at Palenque, the Traditional Theories Began to Look Decidedly Shaky

The "toothache" glyph (left), so called because of the band tied around the head, signifies accession to the throne.

It was while she was working as an artist in Piedras Negras in the 1930s that Tatiana Proskouriakoff noticed how the stelae on this site were divided into groups, each group being associated with a particular building. Later, having discovered the meaning of various glyphs (concerning accession to the throne, the length of reigns, rituals of self-sacrifice, and capture), she succeeded in retracing virtually the whole dynastic history of the site.

There is no longer the slightest doubt: the content of the Maya inscriptions in the documents is historical, and the figures carved on the stelae are the same kings who are named and honored in the texts carved into these monuments.

In tandem with the decoding of the glyphs, progress made in the deciphering of images during the last few years has revealed the central role of the king in Maya ritual and cosmology. To ensure that the world would continue to function correctly, he was required to perform a number of rituals, the complexity of which we are only just beginning to understand. One of the most important and most common was self-sacrifice, involving blood-letting, mutilation, and torture.

The erection of stelae is no longer interpreted as a manifestation of a "cult of time"; instead, these monuments are seen as providing reference points, by establishing a link, at certain fixed periods, between the various calendrical cycles and the dynastic cycle. Indeed, in Maya thought the succession of kings was compared with the solar cycle. In the southeast of the Maya region (Copán, Quiriguá) this concept is illustrated on the monuments themselves; the young king who mounts the throne is the new sun that rises from the jaws of the earth monster; the dead king, whom he succeeds, disappears into the gaping earth.

Until the mid-20th century our knowledge of Maya civilization was very limited, and the hypotheses put forward remained sketchy. Archaeologists of the time could say little about the precise origins of Maya civilization and tended to explain the collapse of the Classic civilization in terms of natural disaster or social unrest: epidemics, earthquakes, revolution, and so on. For each period, they could point to the earliest examples of ceramic vases, stone tools, ball courts, stelae, and carved altars; yet when it came to other aspects, they were far less confident.

Recent research into the areas surrounding the ceremonial centers has shown that around a kernel of large royal, administrative, and religious buildings there were a number of more modest dwellings, largely evidenced by the remains of huts, the whole group constituting a city. Even though there were no streets, and the houses were widely scattered, these communities were urban in the sense that a large proportion of the population was engaged in activities that were non-agricultural: artistic, religious, military, administrative, commercial, and so forth. Even though the largest cities included tens of thousands of inhabitants, there are many smaller sites as well, which may have been either independent or vassals to a larger city. Small towns, villages, hamlets, even isolated farms have all been found.

The images painted on funerary vases usually show mythical scenes from the underworld, some of which can be linked to certain passages in the *Popol Vuh*. Frequently, we find court scenes, in which a high-ranking figure seated on a throne receives homage from his subjects, welcomes warriors (left), or presides over a sacrifice.

The picture they build up is one of a society organized politically into rival city-states, all sharing the same civilization while cultivating their own individual personalities. It was an intensely competitive society, whose history is full of battles, annexations, alliances, and tribute won or lost.

In each of the large cities, whose ruling families were known by emblem glyphs, a king, the equivalent of a god, was responsible before his people for the successful functioning of the universe. To impress both his subjects and his rivals, each ruler tried to live in the most sumptuous palaces, to construct the most lavishly decorated temples on top of the highest pyramids in honor of his ancestors, and to mark his reign in the most striking manner possible by erecting the most impressive monuments.

This struggle for supremacy between the ruling families absorbed more and more of their energies; it also weakened the economy of their kingdoms and wearied the people. In all probability it was this, combined with the decline of agriculture and overpopulation, internal wars and attacks by barbarians, that led to the rapid collapse of the Classic Maya civilization. While the large cities of the

Petén, Chiapas, and Belize had been abandoned and fallen into ruin by the end of the 9th century, Maya civilization managed to survive, more or less, in the Yucatán until the Spanish dealt it the final blow with their dreams of conquest and Christianizing zeal.

And so the remains of this once great civilization lay forgotten—until one day curious explorers visited the Maya ruins, poets wove their dreams around them, and finally scholars pored over them. From their early work derived the romantic vision of a society without a history, a peaceful, profoundly religious society, ignorant of bloody sacrifice. Such fanciful notions have been utterly shattered by recent discoveries. Today we see the Maya in all their frailty: warlike, proud, fallible… but all the more human.

A contemporary Mexican artist painted this class pyramid in the style of the Bonampak murals to illustrate the structure of ancient Maya society. The king, alone and all-powerful, crowns the top tier of the structure, which contains the most important representatives of the ruling dynasty. Below them are the nobles, priests, and warriors. Lower still are the artists, artisans, and traders, some of whom may have had a privileged status at court. Right at the bottom of the scale are the peasants and slaves, the bearers, and the other laborers.

DOCUMENTS

The people who discovered the ruined
cities of the Maya, who unlocked the
secrets of their art and writing, and who
brought the ancient culture to life again

Insights of the First Travelers

The opinions of the earliest visitors to the sites abandoned by the Maya are often surprisingly intuitive for the period. Diego García de Palacio identified the existence of a native Yucatecan people, while Jacinto Garrido was one of the first to suspect that the strange symbols carved on the stelae at Toniná were in fact the characters of a script. History would prove them right.

A Franciscan in Toniná

The writer of the late-19th-century Isagoge Historico Apologetico *gives us a description of the ruins of Toniná after the text of Father Jacinto Garrido, a Franciscan missionary to Toniná in the 1530s, who is said to have described them in his book* Metheores de Aristoteles.

Towards the east of the town of Ocosingo, at a distance of five or six leagues, on the side of a hill which, in that language, is called Aharicab, meaning "hand of the ruler [master, lord, god]" or "the lord of the hands," many and large buildings of great antiquity are to be seen, among which are eight great towers carved with a singular art. On their walls are sculptured many images of men in military dress; their heads covered with steel helmets (*morriones*) with plumes; the body completely dressed in armor to the thighs, and girded with bands; the feet clad in boots reaching to the middle of the leg. This dress is

Jade pendant and plaque carved with images of the sun god, found in Toniná (Late Classic, A.D. 600–900).

Sandstone panel, 2 feet 9 inches long, showing Kan-Xul, the king of Palenque, as a prisoner (Late Classic, early 8th century).

similar to the dress of the statues of Copán, except for the backs, which are girded in bands and not ribbons, like the others.

On a great Plaza at the foot of that same hill there are also many other statues of stone very well carved; but in different dress, as they have on their heads something like crowns of hats which end in a point, but without any brim. The dress is in the style of a sack coat, which is square at the neck, with sleeves which reach to the middle of the arm and are attached to the lower part of the body so that it reaches the middle of the thigh. Around the waist are some ribbons with their *hevillas* [?] all sculptured most curiously in the stone itself. The feet are clad in boots which reach to the middle of the legs. Some statues hold their arms crossed on their breasts; others have them close to their breasts, though not crossed, and without any insignia. In the buildings are also found some shields of stone, hard as flint, which may have a diameter of about five *quartas*, more or less, all of a very even surface and highly polished, and around the edge of each is a border just like an old sexma [coin worth 4 to 5 reales], and all through this are many characters of various figures or ciphers which the P. R. do Fr. Jacinto Garrido says are Chaldean letters.

Many of these shields and statues have been carried to the town of Ocosingo where I have seen them. The

Toniná is less interesting for its architecture than for its sculpture, which uses the local sandstone. A king carrying a ceremonial bar (left), and the most recent Maya stela yet found, dating from A.D. 909.

characters in the border of the shield looked to me more like ciphers of hieroglyphs relating to actions and happenings than like letters, because each of these figures is in a small cartouche (*cassita*) with its outlines distinct from any other, and each cartouche has too much work in it for it to be only one letter, and had they been only letters, not more than one word could have been written on each shield. On one of these shields there is carved in low relief a man of perfect stature, feet and hands tied together with one rope, so artfully enclosed in the circle of that shield that within a diameter of one *vara* one can see all the limbs of a tall man in proper proportion. On this shield it seemed that they wanted to show that they had subdued some great prince or chief of some tribe of Indians, as the man is represented bound, naked, and with hair in the style of the Indians, and seems to have been subdued with violence.

Isagoge Historico Apologetico
1892

Ruins of Copán

During a tour of inspection an important colonial magistrate discovered the ruins of a site that would later be called Copán. His letter to the king of Spain, dated 1576, remained unpublished until 1860.

Near here, on the road to the city of San Pedro, in the first town within the province of Honduras, called Copán, are certain ruins and vestiges of a great population and of superb edifices, of such skill, that it appears they could never have been built by a people as rude as the natives of that province.

One of the six seated figures disposed at regular intervals along the central axis of the Hieroglyphic Stairway in Copán.

They are found on the banks of a beautiful river, in an extensive and well chosen plain, temperate in climate, fertile, and abounding in fish and game.

Among the ruins are mounds which appear to have been built by the hands of men, as well as many other remarkable things. Before reaching them, we find remains of heavy walls, and a great eagle in stone, having on its breast a tablet a yard square, covered with unknown characters.

Arriving at the ruins, we find another stone in the form of a giant, which the ancient Indians aver was the guardian of this sanctuary. Entering the ruins we find a cross of stone, three palms in height, with one of the arms broken off. Further on we encounter ruined edifices, and among them a number of stones sculptured with much skill; also a great statue more than four yards in height, which resembles a bishop in his pontifical robes, with a well-wrought miter on his head, and rings on his fingers.

Near this, is a well built plaza or square, with steps or grades, which, from description, resemble those of the Coliseum at Rome. In some places it has eighty steps, paved, and made in part at least of fine stones, well-worked. In this square are six great statues; three representing men with armor in mosaic, and garters around their legs. Their arms are loaded with ornaments. Two are of women, with long robes, and with headdresses in the Roman style. The remaining statue is of a bishop, who holds in his hands a packet resembling a box or small trunk. It seems that these statues were idols, for in front of each of them is a large stone, in which is carved a small reservoir, with its groove, in which the blood was collected from the sacrifices. We find also the little altars on which the perfumes were burned before them. In the center of the square is a large basin of stone, which appears to have served for baptism; and in which also, sacrifices may have been made in common.

Tufa stela from Copán with the "Eighteen Rabbit" king on the front and inscriptions on the other sides.

After passing this square, we ascend by a great number of steps to a high place, which appears to have been devoted to *mitotes* and other ceremonies; it seems to have been constructed with the greatest care, for throughout we find the stones excellently well-worked. On one side of this structure, is a tower or terrace, very high, and dominating the river which flows at its base. Here a large piece of the wall has fallen, exposing the entrance of two caves or passages, extending under the structure, very long and narrow, and well built. I was not able to discover for what they served, or why they were constructed. There is here a grand stairway descending by a great number of steps, to the river.

Besides these things, there are many others which prove that here was formerly the seat of a great power, and a great population, civilized, and considerably advanced in the arts, as is shown in the various figures and buildings. I endeavored, with all possible care, to ascertain from the Indians, through the traditions derived from the ancients, what people lived here, and what they knew or had heard from their ancestors concerning them. But they have no books relating to their antiquities, nor do I believe that in all this district there is more than one, which I possess.

They say that in ancient times there came from Yucatán a great lord, who built these edifices, but at the end of some years returned to his native country, leaving them entirely deserted. And this is what appears most likely, for tradition says that the people of Yucatán anciently conquered the provinces of Ayajal, Lacandon, Verapaz, Chiquimula, and Copán; and it is certain that the Apay language which is spoken here is current and understood in Yucatán and the aforesaid provinces. It appears also, that these edifices are like those which the first Spaniards discovered in Yucatán and Tabasco, where there were figures of bishops, and of armed men, as well as of crosses. And as such things are found nowhere, except in the aforesaid places, it may well be believed, that the builders of all were of the same origin.

From the aforesaid places I returned to Guatemala, because some of the members of the Audiencia had fallen sick, and it was necessary for the despatch of business. In returning, I passed through places cold and rough, where there are the largest and most beautiful pines and oaks, cedars, cypresses, and many other varieties of trees, which are to be found in these provinces.

These are the most remarkable things which I discovered in this visit which I made, under Your Majesty's orders. I have not recounted all that I learned of the Indians during the time of their infidelity, because it would make volumes; but I can give what I have retained in my memory, if Your Majesty thinks it useful, in such a manner, at least, as to prove my goodwill.

May Our Lord preserve Your Royal and Catholic person for many years, with augmentation of dominion, and with happy deeds. From Your city of Guatemala, March 8th, 1576. Your Royal Catholic Majesty's humble and loyal servant, the licentiate Palacio.

Don Diego García de Palacio
letter to the king of Spain, 1576

Explorers Rediscover a Lost World

It was 1839. An American diplomat, John Lloyd Stephens, and an English painter, Frederick Catherwood, were making their way through the jungle of Central America. Stephens was obsessed by the image of an ancient city buried in the tropical forest. "Of course I believe del Río's report," he assured Catherwood. "And I believe Galindo's tale. I am convinced that neither of them was making it up." Enthusiastic travelers such as Galindo, Stephens, and Charnay were all impassioned observers of a world that was about to be brought back to life.

Ruins of Palenque

These ruins extend for more than twenty miles, along the summit of the ridge which separates the country of the wild Maya Indians…from the state of Chiapas, and must anciently have embraced a city and its suburbs. The principal buildings are erected on the most prominent heights, and to several of them, if not to all, stairs were constructed. From the hollows beneath, the steps, as well as all the vestiges which time has left, are wholly of stone and plaster.

The principal edifice I have discovered, and style the palace, is built in several squares; but the main halls, or galleries, run in a direction from the N.N.E. to the S.S.W. Allowing for the variation of the compass, which is 9 [degrees] E., this position, and its perpendicular, are most exactly observed in all the edifices I have examined, be their situation what it may. This is the more remarkable, as it does not arise from the formation of streets, as no such regular communications existed betwe[e]n the houses. These are formed of galleries eight feet wide, separated by walls a yard thick, and two rows of galleries complete the building: the height of the walls to the eaves is nine feet, and thence three yards more to the top, to which the roofs incline, being covered by horizontal stones a foot wide.… Doors are numerous in all the halls, and the spaces which contained the top beams are exactly preserved in the stone, though the wood-work has entirely disappeared. All the habitations must have been exceedingly dark, if the doors were of wood and kept shut; as the windows, though many, are but small circular and square perforations, and subject to no particular arrangement. Evidently the architects avoided symmetry, not from ignorance but design....

In one of the galleries of the palace is a sort of picture, contained on a stone of an oval shape, about two yards in diameter; the figures are in relievo, and still bear evidence of having been coloured: a female...sits cross-legged on a seat or sofa, which is just large enough to hold her, and has at each end the representation of an animal's head, with a collar round the neck; a person, apparently an old woman, dressed in a tippet and wrapper, both worked like a plaid, presents on her knees, to the sitting female, a human head, adorned with a solitary tuft of feathers....Near this is the principal entrance to the vaults, which run underneath the palace, and which I have explored by candle-light, though much annoyed by the large bats that infest all the ruins....

The whole of the ruins are now buried in a thick forest, and months might be delightfully employed in exploring them. My time is unfortunately limited; but I have seen sufficient to ascertain the high civilisation of their former inhabitants, and that they possessed the art of representing sounds by signs, with which I hitherto believed no Americans previous to the conquest were acquainted.

The neighbouring country, for many leagues distant, contains remains of the ancient labours of its people,—bridges, reservoirs, monumental inscriptions, subterraneous edifices, &c.; but this spot was evidently the capital, and none could be better chosen for the metropolis of a civilised, commercial, and extended nation.... It is strikingly remarkable the almost exact corresponding situation of this country in the new, with that which Egypt held in the Old World....Every thing bears testimony that these surprising people were not physically dissimilar from the present Indians; but their civilisation far surpassed that of the Mexicans and Peruvians: they must have existed long prior to the fourteenth century; since the former, who would have been their neighbours, and not deficient in enterprise and talent, would certainly otherwise have learnt from them the art of writing....

I also presume that the Maya language is derived from them: it is still spoken by all the Indians, and even by most of the other inhabitants through-out Yucatán, the district of Petén, and the eastern part of Tabasco....

With regard to the present inhabitants of these regions, the wild Indians to the south are an uncivilised and timid tribe... and the subdued Indians who inhabit the states of Chiapas and Tabasco are equally in a low scale of improvement. When asked who built these edifices, they reply, "The devil!" A pretty village, styled Palenque, and which has had the honour of giving its name to these ruins, was built about a century ago, six miles to the northeast....I inquired of the priest and alcalde, as the oracles of Palenque, who they supposed were the builders of these ancient edifices. The priest shook his head, and hinted at their being antediluvian! while the alcalde stoutly affirmed that they must have been built by a colony of Spaniards prior to the conquest!!!

Juan Galindo
Letter to the London *Literary Gazette*
October 1831

Trials of Photography in the Tropics

With the automatic cameras we have today it is generally thought that "any idiot can take a photograph." In the days of Désiré Charnay it took almost as much preparation and hard work to photograph a monument as it did to draw it.

In Uxmal I experienced countless difficulties in my operations; the terrible heat, decomposition of the chemicals, and all kinds of accidents almost compromised the success of my expedition. Add to that a series of sleepless nights, and you will have some idea of my position.

I have said that I set up camp in the Nunnery palace, and that I turned one of the rooms of the south wing into my bedroom. The first night I spent there was blissful; I had removed the hangings that covered the doorway, and the swinging of my hammock helped to make the heat almost bearable.

I slept alone in the palace, as the Indians refused point-blank to spend the night among the ruins; the very idea inspired them with mortal terror. Antonio [Charnay's guide?] had begged me to return to the *hacienda* each night, but this would have been a waste of time, and as I could guess what he was driving at, I left him free to sleep wherever he wished, providing he and the Indians were there ready, at my disposal, by daybreak....I was therefore alone, and thanks to my labors, I had scarcely lain down in my hammock before I fell into a deep sleep.

On the third day I lost this sweet rest for good. At around four in the afternoon there had been a dreadful storm, accompanied by torrential rain. Unable to take my evening stroll, I was limited to taking a few notes, sitting by the door to my lodgings. Night fell and I settled into my hammock, where I quickly fell fast asleep. But alas! it was not to last, for I was suddenly awoken by dreadful pain. The sound of wings filled the room, and feeling around

Charnay taking photographs in the jungle. Right: The photographer poses in front of the ruins of Aké (Yucatán).

myself I found a multitude of cold flat insects the size of a large cockroach. It was horrific! Several of them were walking over my face; I hurriedly lit a candle, and my eyes were struck by the most revolting scene imaginable.

Over two hundred of the dreadful creatures lay trapped in my hammock, as if caught in a net; at least thirty of the animals were still attached to me, and I quickly shook them off; my face, hands, and body were covered with swellings that were unbearably painful.

Several of the insects lying in the hammock were fat and swollen with the blood they had sucked from me; the walls were covered with their companions, who seemed to be waiting until their friends, once sated, would allow them to take their turn. How on earth could I rid myself of so many enemies?

I armed myself with a short plank of wood and embarked on the massacre. It was an appalling and disgusting task, which made me feel quite sick. The battle lasted two hours; without pity, without mercy, I squashed every one. Once I was sure that the place was clean, that there were only dead bodies left, I hermetically sealed the door and tried to go back to sleep; but two hours later I had to repeat the whole procedure. These insects were *piques*, or flying bugs. The next day I changed my place of residence, but my enemies hounded me down there as well, and my life became a living hell....

I found I had less energy for my work, and my strength was further sapped by appalling sweating.... Each picture could take me up to two or three attempts; some, which were perfectly successful, were lost through unexpected accidents and often as a result of the Indians' indiscreet curiosity; in spite of my express instructions, they could not keep their hands off the finished shots that I left to dry out of doors. One example of this is illustrated by the following incident, which almost prevented me from photographing the most beautiful of the palaces, the House of the Governor. I had kept it until last, so as to be able to devote all my attention to it. As the palace stands on a pyramid, I had had to construct a drystone base 12 feet high on the platform in front of it, in order to raise my camera to the level of the building. As my darkroom, which I had set up in the large central chamber, was 260 feet from the place where the plate would be exposed, I was forced to shroud all my equipment in damp cloths; I wrapped some around the camera frame so that the layer of collodion would not dry out during the long exposure time and all the comings and goings. And to keep the time as short as possible I ran.

Because the palace is very large, I decided to photograph it in two halves, so as to capture it in greater detail and to achieve a more striking overall effect. For these pictures I had set aside a

bottle of collodion that had been left to settle out perfectly; I was relying on this and on two glass plates, which were the only ones I had been able to find. I had no more chemicals left, and no more glass plates, so I had to get it right, and get it right twice in quick succession, in case the light should change, making the lighting different for each half of the monument.

So I began, and the first shot worked perfectly: not a mark, clear, transparent, each detail properly highlighted—in a word, irreproachable.

For the second, a ray of light got into the camera, leaving a black line across the glass and making the shot impossible. I quickly cleaned the glass plate; my collodion was running low and I had none in reserve, so I poured it out as carefully as possible. Aware of how I had accidentally spoiled the first shot, I found it quite easy to avoid making the same mistake twice. All went well; the shot was successful; it had the same tone, the same clarity, and I was already glorying in my successful handling of such a delicate operation.

I put down the plate I had just finished to examine the first one again, so as to get a better idea of the quality of my results. I held the transparent plate in my hand, and looking through it, I went to wipe away some films of chemical that I could see on the back of the glass. O despair! someone had turned the glass plate over, and my whole hand wiped across the exposed layer of collodion. I knew that the whole thing was utterly ruined and, looking fiercely around me, uttering dreadful curses, I demanded to know who was responsible. The guilty party was careful not to confess. The intensity of my fury made me leap

around like a tiger, and the Indians looked petrified. What could I do? In the Nunnery palace I had left several bottles containing leftover sensitized collodion. I promised a piastre to the first man who could bring them to me.

The poor things rushed away with the speed of arrows, setting off on a frenzied steeplechase along the route we had hacked through the forest. In my rage I could scarcely tolerate the delay, but I hurried to clean the glass plate once more, and they were back even before I had finished. Out of the three runners there were four winners, as each one presented me with a bottle....

Désiré Charnay
Cités et ruines américaines, 1863

A Precarious Situation

Throughout the 19th century Stephens' Incidents of Travel *volumes were some of the best-selling books on exploration. This was due both to the fascinating subject matter and his fine style.*

We had brought the *silla* with us merely as a measure of precaution, with[out] much expectation of being obliged to use it; but at a steep pitch, which made my head almost burst to think of climbing, I resorted to it for the first time. It was a large, clumsy armchair, put together with wooden pins and bark strings. The Indian who was to carry me, like all the others, was small, not more than five feet seven, very thin, but symmetrically formed. A bark strap was tied to the arms of the chair, and, sitting down, he placed his back against the back of the chair, adjusted the length of the strings, and smoothed the bark across his forehead with a little cushion to relieve the pressure. An Indian on each side lifted it up, and the carrier rose on his feet, stood still a moment, threw me up once or twice to adjust me on his shoulders, and set off with one man on each side. It was a great relief, but I could feel every movement, even to the heaving of his chest. The ascent was one of the steepest on the whole road. In a few minutes he stopped and sent forth a sound, usual with Indian carriers, between a whistle and a blow, always painful to my ears, but which I never felt so disagreeably before. My face was turned backward; I could not see where he was going, but observed that the Indian on the left fell back. Not to increase the labor of carrying me, I sat as still as possible; but in a few minutes, looking over my shoulder, saw that we

were approaching the edge of a precipice more than a thousand feet deep. Here I became very anxious to dismount; but I could not speak intelligibly, and the Indians could or would not understand my signs.... I remained until he put me down of his own accord. The poor fellow was wet with perspiration, and trembled in every limb. Another stood ready to take me up, but I had had enough.... It was bad enough to see an Indian toiling with a dead weight on his back; but to feel him trembling under one's own body, hear his hard breathing, see the sweat rolling down him, and feel the insecurity of the position, made this a mode of traveling which nothing but constitutional laziness and insensibility could endure....

We could not understand how far it was to Nopa, our intended stopping

One of Catherwood's drawings of his expedition with Stephens.

place, which we supposed to be on the top of the mountain. To every question the Indians answered *una legua*. Thinking it could not be much higher, we continued. For an hour more we had a very steep ascent, and then commenced a terrible descent. At this time the sun had disappeared; dark clouds overhung the woods, and thunder rolled heavily on top of the mountain. As we descended a heavy wind swept through the forest; the air was filled with dry leaves; branches were snapped and broken, trees bent, and there was every appearance of a violent tornado. To hurry down on foot was out of the question. We were so tired that it was impossible; and, afraid of being caught on the mountain by a hurricane and deluge of rain, we spurred down as fast as we could go. It was a continued descent, without any relief, stony, and very steep.… Fortunately for the reader, this is our last mountain, and I can end honestly with a climax: it was the worst mountain I ever encountered in that or any other country, and, under our apprehension of the storm, I will venture to say that no travelers ever descended in less time. At a quarter before five we reached the plain. The mountain was hidden by clouds, and the storm was now raging above us. We crossed a river, and continuing along it through a thick forest, reached the rancho of Nopa.

Explorations in Copán

We ascended by large stone steps, in some places perfect, and in others thrown down by trees which had grown up between the crevices, and reached a terrace, the form of which was impossible to make out, from the density of the forest in which it was

enveloped. Our guide cleared a way with his machete, and we passed, as it lay half buried in the earth, a large fragment of stone elaborately sculptured, and came to the angle of a structure with steps on the sides, in form and appearance, so far as the trees would enable us to make it out, like the sides of a pyramid. Diverging from the

base, and working our way through the thick woods, we came upon a square stone column, about fourteen feet high and three feet on each side, sculptured in very bold relief, and on all four of the sides, from the base to the top. The front was the figure of a man curiously and richly dressed, and the face, evidently a portrait, solemn, stern, and well fitted to excite terror. The back was of a different design, unlike anything we had ever seen before, and the sides were covered with hieroglyphics. This our guide called an "Idol"; and before it, at a distance of three feet, was a large block of stone, also sculptured with figures and emblematical devices, which he called an altar. The sight of

A broken "idol" in Copán, engraved by Catherwood.

this unexpected monument put at rest at once and forever, in our minds, all uncertainty in regard to the character of American antiquities, and gave us the assurance that the objects we were in search of were interesting, not only as the remains of an unknown people, but as works of art, proving, like newly discovered historical records, that the people who once occupied the continent of America were not savages.

With an interest perhaps stronger than we had ever felt in wandering among the ruins of Egypt, we followed our guide, who, sometimes missing his way, with constant and vigorous use of his machete, conducted us through the thick forest, among half-buried fragments, to fourteen monuments of the same character and appearance, some with more elegant designs, and some in workmanship equal to the finest monuments of the Egyptians; one displaced from its pedestal by enormous roots; another locked in the close embrace of branches of trees, and almost lifted out of the earth; another hurled to the ground, and bound down by huge vines and creepers; and one standing, with its altar before it, seemingly to shade and shroud it as a sacred thing; in the solemn stillness of the woods, it seemed a divinity mourning over a fallen people.

The only sounds that disturbed the quiet of this buried city were the noise of monkeys moving among the tops of the trees, and the cracking of dry branches broken by their weight. They moved over our heads in long and swift processions, forty or fifty at a time, some with little ones wound in their long arms, walking out to the end of boughs, and holding on with their hind feet or a curl of the tail, sprang to a branch of the next tree, and, with a noise like a current of wind, passed on into the depths of the forest. It was the first time we had seen these mockeries of humanity, and, with the strange monuments around us, they seemed like wandering spirits of the departed race guarding the ruins of their former habitations.…

At daylight the clouds still hung over the forest; as the sun rose they cleared away; our workmen made their appearance, and at nine o'clock we left the hut. The branches of the trees were dripping wet, and the ground very muddy. Trudging once more over the district which contained the principal monuments,we were startled by the immensity of the work before us, and very soon we concluded that to explore the whole extent would be impossible. Our guides knew only of this district; but having seen columns beyond the village, a league distant, we had reason to believe that others were strewed in different directions, completely buried in the woods, and entirely unknown. The woods were so dense that it was almost hopeless to think of penetrating them. The only way to make a thorough exploration would be to cut down the whole forest and burn the trees. This was incompatible with our immediate purposes, might be considered taking liberties, and could only be done in the dry season. After deliberation, we resolved first to obtain drawings of the sculptured columns. Even in this there was great difficulty. The designs were very complicated, and so different from anything Mr. Catherwood had ever seen before as to be perfectly unintelligible. The cutting was in very high relief, and required a strong body of light to bring up the figures; and the foliage was so thick, and the shade so deep, that drawing was impossible.

After much consultation, we selected one of the "idols," and determined to cut down the trees around it, and thus lay it open to the rays of the sun. Here again was difficulty. There was no axe; and the only instrument which the Indians possessed was the machete, or chopping-knife, which varies in form in different sections of the country; wielded with one hand, it was useful in clearing away shrubs and branches, but almost harmless upon large trees; and the Indians, as in the days when the Spaniards discovered them, applied to

C atherwood's drawing of an "idol," today known as stela I, half buried in the roots of a tree.

work without ardor, carried it on with little activity, and, like children, were easily diverted from it. One hacked into a tree, and, when tired, which happened very soon, sat down to rest, and another relieved him. While one worked there were always several looking on. I remembered the ring of the woodman's axe in the forests at home, and wished for a few long-sided Green Mountain boys. But we had been buffeted into patience, and watched the Indians while they hacked with their machetes, and even wondered that they succeeded so well....

It is impossible to describe the interest with which I explored these ruins. The ground was entirely new; there were no guidebooks or guides; the whole was a virgin soil. We could not see ten yards before us, and never knew what we should stumble upon next. At one time we stopped to cut away branches and vines which concealed the face of a monument, and then to dig around and bring to light a fragment, a sculptured corner of which protruded from the earth. I leaned over with breathless anxiety while the Indians worked, and an eye, an ear, a foot, or a hand was disentombed; and when the machete rang against the chiseled stone, I pushed the Indians away, and cleared out the loose earth with my hands. The beauty of the sculpture, the solemn stillness of the woods, disturbed only by the scrambling of monkeys and the chattering of parrots, the desolation of the city, and the mystery that hung over it, all created an interest higher, if possible, than I had ever felt among the ruins of the Old World.

John L. Stephens,
Incidents of Travel in Central America, Chiapas, and Yucatán, 1841

Cracking the Code

For centuries people wrestled with the problem. But in vain: the symbols carved in the stone stelae and temples remained unintelligible. Little by little experts began to understand certain glyphs—first individual dates, then the calendar cycles. Only during the last twenty years or so have researchers perfected a method for deciphering the Maya script, based on a proper Maya syntax. A veil has been lifted from what was for centuries the central mystery of the Maya.

Important Historical and Philological Discovery

Constantine Samuel Rafinesque (1783–1840), a prolific writer on myriad subjects from botany to banking, developed an interest in American antiquities in the early 1820s. His letter to the Saturday Evening Post, *addressed to the prominent philologist P. S. Duponceau, which appeared on 13 January 1827, is the first known interpretative work in print dealing with ancient Maya hieroglyphic writing.*

I have the pleasure to announce and communicate to you, that during the course of my present researches into the history of America, I have been successful in discovering the existence of several ancient Alphabetical Glyphic Inscriptions, belonging to this continent.

The wonderful discoveries lately made in Europe by Champollin [sic] and others, relating to the Alphabetical Inscriptions of Egypt and Persia, have led to important results. Your actual attempts to reduce the Chinese characters, to primitive Alphabetical or syllabic elements, evince that much is yet to be learned of the ancient modes of expressing and communicating ideas.

My late discovery will form another link in the chain of philological investigation, and become a very important auxiliary in our historical researches. I allude principally to the inscriptions on the ruins of the ancient city of OTOLUM, near PALENQUE, near CHIAPA, one of the primitive cities of America, whose ruins are 32 miles in circumference! They have been partly made known by a work of Del Río and Cabrera, published in 1822;

but so imperfectly, that a high reward is offered in France, for an account more perfect. Meantime it is from the plates of Del Río, that I have been enabled already to ascertain the nature of the characters inscribed in the walls of this AMERICAN THEBES, to reduce them to their alphabetical elements, and read many of them....

The characters of OTOLUM are totally different from any other we are acquainted with....

Comparing them with the Chinese characters, that are groups of plain rectilinear elements; or the Persian, that form rows of lines; or the Egyptian, that seem rows of distinct figures, & c. I found unity of purpose, but no identity nor similarity of execution.

Searching throughout the whole of the ancient Alphabets for this similarity, I found none that offered the curvilinear elements of the OTOLUM characters, except the OLD LIBYAN.... This Alphabet (one of the most ancient, since it may have been that of the Atlantes or Getulians, the ancestors of the actual Berbers) is quite symbolical, like the Egyptian phonetic....It is in this philosophical Alphabet, that I found the elements of the OTOLUM characters and inscriptions. But the letters, instead of being rows, form compact groups, each group being a word, or short sentence.

All the Libyan *letters* or *symbols*, are found; but they are sometimes modified or ornamented: these ornaments and additions increase the difficulty of reading them, which is very great, owing to the modes of ascertaining the succession of the letters in the groups—however, the main letters are generally larger, and succeed each other from right to left. Appearances of syllabic combinations are often evident, and numbers are perspicuously delineated by long ellipsoids marking 10 with little balls for unities, standing apart.

These OTOLUM characters are totally different from the Azteca or Mexican paintings, which are true symbols, and also from every other American mode of expressing ideas by carvings, paintings, or quipus. They appear besides to belong to a peculiar language, distinct from the Azteca, probably the TZENDAL (called also Chontal, Celtal, &c.), yet spoken from Chiapas to Panama, and connected with the Maya of Yucatán....

Thus we have another clue to our historical and philological researches: The Empire of OTOLUM in central America, founded on the river Tulija, by the Dynasty of Vutan, who perhaps were the NEITON (Neptunes) of North Africa and South Europe, and a branch of Atlantes or Hetulians or Autololes, will become interesting to study. The statues of OTOLUM represent a peculiar race of men with large aquiline noses, thick lips, and conical heads, and appear different from most of the actual American tribes. They were one of the numerous colonies established in America in ancient times, and who brought with them the civilization, language, arts, sciences, & c. of primitive antiquity. Whence the striking analogies detected between the ancient Etruscans, Egyptians, Persians, Turanians, Hindoos, & c. and the polished nations of America; namely, the Mexicans, Peruvians, Muhircas, Chilians, Apalachians, Haytians, Mayans, Utatlans, and Otolans.

C. S. Rafinesque
Letter, *Saturday Evening Post*, 1827

Maya Arithmetic and the Maya Calendar

Today the Western world uses a positional system of arithmetic; this means that, in our decimal system, when any number is read from right to left, each figure has a value ten times greater than the previous figure in the sequence. For example, in 1987, there are 7 units, 8 tens, 9 hundreds, and 1 thousand.

The Maya used a similar system, but the sequence progressed from the bottom upwards, with each level twenty times greater than the one below (base 20, or a vigesimal system). Numbers were written with a bar for a value of five and a dot for each unit. To write 1987, therefore, there would be a bar and two dots at the bottom (= 7), then three bars and four points (19 x 20 = 380), and finally four points at the top (4 x 400 = 1600):

400s level	••••	= 1600
20s level	••••	
	———	
	———	= 380
units	••	
	———	= 7
		————
		1987

Numbers were also expressed in the form of head-shaped glyphs.

The Maya calendar used various separate cycles, the most important of which were:

—The *tzolkin*, or ritual and divinatory calendar, in which the days were indicated by both a number (from 1 to 13) and a named day (twenty in all). The cycle lasted a total of 260 days (13 x 20), after which it was repeated.

—The *haab*, or vague year (so called because it was a quarter day short of the solar year), made up of 365 days divided into eighteen months of twenty days each, with a short "month" of five days at the end of the year.

—The great cycle of 5200 *tuns*. The zero date of the present era, which comprises the entire history of the Maya, probably corresponds to 13 August 3114 b.c. in our own calendar. In this Long Count, as it is known, they calculated the number of *baktuns* (periods of 400 *tuns*), *katuns* (20 *tuns*), *tuns* (360, rather than 365 days), *uinals* (20-day months) and *kins* (days) that had elapsed since the zero date. In the transcription system adopted by Mayanists, a Long Count date would

The "Panel of the Ninety-Six Glyphs" relates the

be written, for example, 9.13.17.15.12 5 *eb* 15 *mac*—or 9 *baktuns*, 13 *katuns*, 17 *tuns*, 15 *uinals* and 12 *kins*, 5 *eb* (*tzolkin* date), and 15 *macs* (*haab* date).

The Leiden Plaque

The Leiden Plaque is a celt, part of a royal costume, which, like the Maya stelae, carries both an image and a hieroglyphic inscription. Today both are relatively well understood by scholars.

Carved from a light green, translucent jade, the Leiden Plaque was a celt from a royal belt-head assemblage. The front surface is polished to a smooth finish and incised with the portrait of a Maya king [Balam-Ahau-Chaan?] in the act of acceding to office. He stands dressed in the regalia of kings, holding a Double-headed Serpent Bar as the sign of his rank. Behind him, a victim who will be sacrificed in rites that sanctify the accession, struggles on his belly looking back across his shoulder.

The carving is an excellent example of Early Classic style and the high craftsmanship of Maya art. The image is tightly packed with an array of symbols that define kingly rank. He is posed stiffly with the head in profile, the shoulder front view, and the legs in profile but separated, so that the detail of both cuffs is clearly visible. In Early Classic art, the clear transfer of symbolic information took precedence over the natural presentation of the human figure. An inscription on the

f four kings of Palenque. Almost half of the characters in this inscription are calendrical.

rear surface…records the date, action, and actor of the scene.

The clothing worn by Balam-Ahau-Chaan became the most sacred costume of kings; to put it on for the first time was to become king. Because of its central importance in Maya kingship, we present a detailed examination of the Leiden figure, isolating the parts to view each component unimpeded.

The king stands in side view with his shoulders turned toward the viewer so that the objects he wears and holds can be easily seen. He wears a backrack, which emerges from behind his shoulder. A thick collar with a human head attached to the front is tied around his neck. He wears a cloth skirt with a beaded and fringed edge surmounted with a belt with the Jaguar God of the Underworld, crossed bands and disks, and a belt and celt assemblage on the right front side. An elaborate loin ornament dangles to his knees. He wears cuffs on his wrists and anklets constructed of leather bands tied through jade disks into bows. He wears sandals of the Early Classic style.

The royal belt overlays the cloth skirt and the Jaguar God of the Underworld at his front waist. The side head appears to be mounted on the rear of the belt, but its position was shifted so that it would appear fully in profile view, rather than foreshortened. A chain drops from the belt to a personification head with a jade ornament hanging from its mouth.

The headdress, like the belt, is a critical part of the costume. It was constructed on a cap lined with jade cylinders and beads. A side flange was built on either side of the head so that the weight of the heavy jade flares would be supported by the headdress,

The Leiden Plaque (recto)

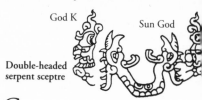

God K

Sun God

Double-headed serpent sceptre

Graphic interpretation of the Leiden Plaque (rec

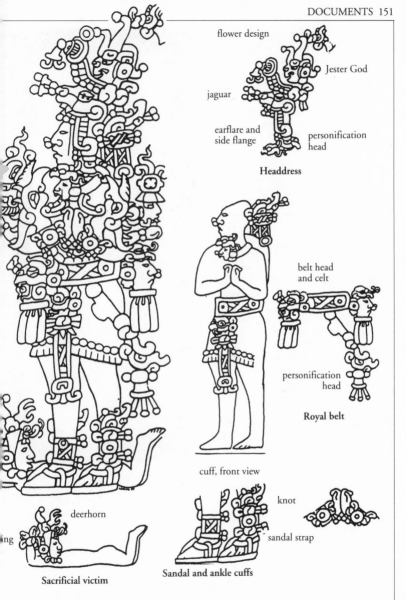

flower design

Jester God

jaguar

earflare and
side flange

personification
head

Headdress

belt head
and celt

personification
head

Royal belt

cuff, front view

deerhorn

ing

knot

sandal strap

Sacrificial victim

Sandal and ankle cuffs

The individual drawings are components of the large main drawing.

rather than the earlobes. The main head is a naturalistic jaguar with nose ornaments extending in front of his muzzle. He wears a jade headband culminating in a flower design, perhaps a morning glory.

The king holds his arms against his chest in a position that naturally occurs when an object is held in the crook of the arms and against the chest. This position became the standardized way to hold the Double-headed Serpent Bar, the most important scepter of Maya kings. Sometimes shown with a rigid bar or a naturalistic serpent body between the two heads, the scepter terminates with gaping serpent mouths from which emerge the gods who sanctify the king's position. [In this case] God K is on the right and the Sun God on the left.

Positioned on his stomach behind the ruler's feet, a bound captive struggles, anticipating his sacrifice in the accession ritual. A decorated *ahau* on his head marks the noble captive as a lord. He wears a large earflare, and his head, turned to look back, is tied vertically by a cloth.

THE INSCRIPTION

The Leiden Plaque date, 8.14.3.1.12 1 *eb* O *yaxkin*, or September 17 A.D. 320, occupies the first ten glyph blocks of the text; the action and actor occupy the last five....

The first glyph, the Initial Series Introductory Glyph, simply announces that a Long Count date is coming. The main sign is a "drum," read *tun*, and the head above it is the Sun God, the patron of *yaxkin*, the month into which this date falls.

The next five glyphs are composed of numbers and the signs for the cycles that are being counted, but in this very rare

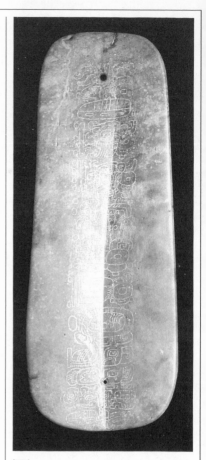

The Leiden Plaque (verso).

format, the glyphs for the *baktun* (400 years) and the *katun* (20 years) are exchanged. Eight, the first number, is followed by the *katun* "bird," recording "eight 400-year cycles." The next glyph includes the number 14 and the *baktun* "bird head," recording "fourteen 20-year cycles." The third

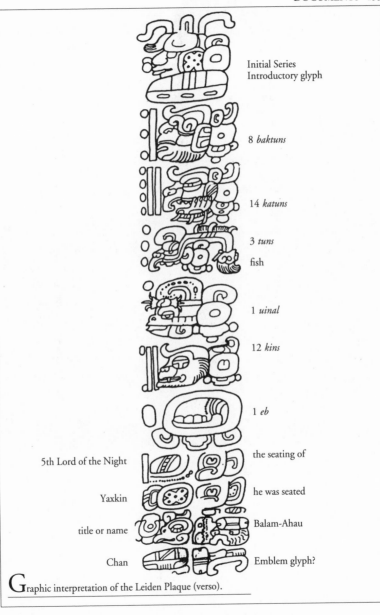

Initial Series
Introductory glyph

8 *baktuns*

14 *katuns*

3 *tuns*

fish

1 *uinal*

12 *kins*

1 *eb*

5th Lord of the Night — the seating of

Yaxkin — he was seated

title or name — Balam-Ahau

Chan — Emblem glyph?

Graphic interpretation of the Leiden Plaque (verso).

Tikal: temple I, the central acropolis and stelae, seen from the north acropolis.

component has the number 3 and the personification, or god, of the *tun* (the 360-day year), recording "three years." This *tun* glyph is particularly wonderful: it is a fish-dragon with a water scroll on its head and a fishfin on its spine; a fish is nibbling on the tail. In iconic form, this is the Water-Lily Fish Monster.

Together, the first three parts of this date record that eight groups of 400 years (3200), fourteen groups of 20 years (280), plus three years—for a total of 3483 years—have passed since the zero date of the Maya calendar. Remember that in the Maya system, the year, or *tun*, has only 360 days.

The next two glyphs record the number of months and days that had elapsed in the next year. This is confusing to those accustomed to the Christian calendar, because for us the day after New Year's Day in the first year was January 2, A.D. 1. We have no zero year, but the Maya did. Their calendar works much like the way we record our ages: a child is not one year old until a year after birth. The Leiden Plaque records that the era was 3483 *tuns* old. In the next year, one *uinal* (month) and twelve days had passed. The Leiden date occurred on the thirty-second (20 + 12) day of the 3484th *tun* of the Maya era.

The glyphs recording the twenty-day month and the day are also worth noting. The *uinal* is personified by a toad monster with a water scroll atop his head, while the personification of the day is Hun-Chuen, the howler monkey god of writing....

Thus, the first six glyphs on the Leiden Plaque record the day as the time elapsed since the zero year in a system. The next four glyphs tell us what this day is called in the repetitive [short] cycles.... [The first] records 8.14.3.1.12 after the zero date, the day 1 *eb* is reached in the 260-day *tzolkin* cycle.

[The next glyph] records that on this day, the fifth of the nine Lords of the Night was in power. This date happens to fall on the 120th day of the *haab* [of 365 days] or the 20th day of *xul* [one of the eighteen months of the *haab*]. In this instance, the scribe elected to call this day the "seating of *yaxkin*," the next month: [the third glyph] is *chum*, "seating," and [the fourth] is *yaxkin*.

To summarize, the calendric information tells us that the patron of *yaxkin* was in power; that eight *baktuns*, fourteen *katuns*, three *tuns*, one *uinal*

and twelve days had ended since the zero date; that this day fell on 1 *eb* in the *tzolkin*; that the fifth Lord of the Night was in office; and that on this day, the month *yaxkin* was seated in the 365-day *haab*. In a more convenient system, using our own numbers, we write this day 8.14.3.1.12 1 *eb* G5 O *yaxkin*; in our calendar, it was Friday in the cycle of seven weekdays, September 17 in the cycle of the tropical year, and in the 320th year of the present era—or Friday, September 17, A.D. 320.

The last five glyphs concern the action and the actor.] The verb is "he was seated," identifying the scene on the other side [of the plaque] as accession. The second glyph is either the office into which this person was seated or it is part of his name. The next pair of glyphs name the new king with an *ahau* [lord] glyph half-covered by jaguar pelt and an unknown head variant followed by the "sky" *chaan* sign. Using the readable parts of the name, we can tentatively call him Balam [jaguar]-Ahau-Chaan.

The last glyph also occurs on Tikal Stela 4, dated 59 years later, in the position usually occupied by Emblem Glyphs. Since the provenance of Stela 4 is clear, the presence of the same glyph on the Leiden Plaque has been taken as evidence that it was manufactured at Tikal. However, the inscriptions of Tikal record that a ruler named Jaguar Paw was ruling that city both three years earlier and 56 years later than the Leiden date. If these two royal names refer to the same person, then Tikal was ruled by someone else when this accession took place, and the Leiden Plaque comes from another city.

Linda Schele and Mary E. Miller,
Adapted from
The Blood of Kings, 1986

The Quiché Maya's Book of Counsel

The Popol Vuh *is a collection of myths and traditional stories handed down orally over generations by the Quiché Maya, who lived for centuries on the high plateaus of Honduras and Guatemala. When the Spanish Franciscan friars encountered the Quiché Maya in the 17th century the* Popol Vuh *came to be transcribed in Latin script.*

[After Hunahpu and Xbalanque were born,] "Throw them out of here! They're really loudmouths!" said the grandmother.

After that, when they put them on an anthill, they slept soundly there. And when they removed them from there, they put them in brambles next.

And this is what [their elder brothers] One Monkey [Hun Chuen] and One Artisan [Hun Batz] wanted: that they should die on the anthill and die in the brambles. One Monkey and One Artisan wanted this because they were rowdyish and flushed with jealousy. They didn't allow their younger brothers in the house at first, as if they didn't even know them, but even so they flourished in the mountains.

And One Monkey and One Artisan were great flautists and singers, and as they grew up they went through great suffering and pain. It had cost them suffering to become great knowers. Through it all they became flautists, singers and writers, carvers. They did everything well. They simply knew it when they were born, they simply had genius. And they were the successors of their fathers who had gone to Xibalba [Hell], their dead fathers.

Since One Monkey and One Artisan were great knowers, in their hearts they already realized everything when their younger brothers came into being, but they didn't reveal their insight because of their jealousy. The anger in their hearts came down on their own heads; no great harm was done. They were decoyed by Hunahpu and Xbalanque, who merely went out shooting every day. These two got no love from the grandmother, or from One Monkey and One Artisan. They weren't given their meals; the meals had been prepared, and One Monkey and One Artisan had already eaten them before they got there.

But Hunahpu and Xbalanque aren't turning red with anger; rather, they just let it go, even though they know their proper place, which they see as clear as day. So they bring birds when they arrive each day, and One Monkey and One Artisan eat them. Nothing whatsoever is given to Hunahpu and Xbalanque, either one of them. All One Monkey and One Artisan do is play and sing.

And then Hunahpu and Xbalanque arrived again, but now they came in here without bringing their birds, so the grandmother turned red:

"What's your reason for not bringing birds?" Hunahpu and Xbalanque were asked.

"There are some, our dear grandmother, but our birds just got hung up in a tree," they said, "and there's no way to get up the tree after them, our dear grandmother, and so we'd like our elder brothers to please go with us, to please go get the birds down," they said.

"Very well. We'll go with you at dawn," the elder brothers replied.

Now they had won, and they gathered their thoughts, the two of them, about the fall of One Monkey and One Artisan:

"We'll just turn their very being around with our words. So be it, since they have caused us great suffering. They wished that we might die and disappear—we, their younger brothers.

This canoe trip undertaken by gods and animals, engraved on a bone from Tikal, illustrates a myth that has not survived.

Just as they wished us to be slaves here, so we shall defeat them there. We shall simply make a sign of it," they said to one another.

And then they went there beneath a tree, the kind named yellowwood, together with the elder brothers. When they got there they started shooting. There were countless birds up in the tree, chittering, and the elder brothers were amazed when they saw the birds. And not one of these birds fell down beneath the tree:

"Those birds of ours don't fall down; just go throw them down," they told their elder brothers.

"Very well," they replied.

And then they climbed up the tree, and the tree began to grow, its trunk got thicker.

After that, they wanted to get down, but now One Monkey and One Artisan couldn't make it down from the tree. So they said, from up in the tree:

"How can we grab hold? You, our younger brothers, take pity on us! Now this tree looks frightening to us, dear younger brothers," they said from up in the tree. Then Hunahpu and Xbalanque told them:

"Undo your pants, tie them around your hips, with the long end trailing like a tail behind you, and then you'll be better able to move," they were told by their younger brothers.

"All right," they said.

And then they left the ends of their loincloths trailing, and all at once these became tails. Now they looked like mere monkeys.

After that they went along in the trees of the mountains, small and great. They went through the forests, now howling, now keeping quiet in the branches of the trees.

Such was the defeat of One Monkey and One Artisan by Hunahpu and Xbalanque. They did it by means of their genius alone.

And when they got home they said, when they came to their grandmother and mother:

"Our dear grandmother, something has happened to our elder brothers. They've become simply shameless, they're like animals now," they said.

"If you've done something to your elder brothers, you've knocked me down and stood me on my head. Please don't do anything to your elder brothers, my dear grandchildren," the grandmother said to Hunahpu and Xbalanque. And they told their grandmother:

"Don't be sad, our dear grandmother. You will see the faces of our elder brothers again. They'll come, but this will be a test for you, our dear grandmother. Will you please not laugh while we test their destiny?" they said.

And then they began playing. They played "Hunahpu Monkey."

And then they sang, they played, they drummed. When they took up their flutes and drums, their grandmother sat down with them, then they played, they sounded out the tune, the song that got its name then. "Hunahpu Monkey" is the name of the tune.

And then One Monkey and One Artisan came back, dancing when they arrived.

And then, when the grandmother looked, it was their ugly faces the grandmother saw. Then she laughed, the grandmother could not hold back her laughter, so they just left right away, out of her sight again, they went

A spider monkey, the tutelary god of artists and scribes, is painted on this broad open bowl.

up and away in the forest.

"Why are you doing that, our dear grandmother? We'll only try four times; only three times are left. We'll call them with the flute, with song. Please hold back your laughter. We'll try again," said Hunahpu and Xbalanque.

Next they played again, then they [One Monkey and One Artisan] came back, dancing again, they arrived again, in the middle of the patio of the house. As before, what they did was delightful; as before, they tempted their grandmother to laugh. Their grandmother laughed at them soon enough. The monkeys looked truly ridiculous, with the skinny little things below their bellies and their tails wiggling in front of their breasts. When they came back the grandmother had to laugh at them, and they went back into the mountains.

"Please, why are you doing that, our dear grandmother? Even so, we'll try it a third time now," said Hunahpu and Xbalanque.

Again they played, again they came dancing, but their grandmother held back her laughter. Then they climbed up here, cutting right across the building, with thin red lips, with faces blank, puckering their lips, wiping their mouths and faces, suddenly scratching

themselves. And when the grandmother saw them again, the grandmother burst out laughing again, and again they went out of sight because of the grandmother's laughter.

"Even so, our dear grandmother, we'll get their attention."

So for the fourth time they called on the flute, but they didn't come back again. The fourth time they went straight into the forest. So they told their grandmother:

"Well, we've tried, our dear grandmother. They came at first, and we've tried calling them again. So don't be sad. We're here—we, your grandchildren. Just love our mother, dear grandmother. Our elder brothers will be remembered. So be it: they have lived here and they have been named; they are to be called One Monkey and One Artisan," said Hunahpu and Xbalanque.

So they were prayed to by the flautists and singers among the ancient people, and the writers and carvers prayed to them. In ancient times they turned into animals, they became monkeys, because they just magnified themselves, they abused their younger brothers. Just as they wished them to be slaves, so they themselves were brought low.

Ancient Maya, Modern Maya

One of the attractions of Maya research is the satisfying continuity between their pagan past and their syncretistic present. The Maya of today have preserved most of their ancient customs; they remember the old myths about the creation of the world and the deeds of the gods. In their prayers they continue to name the ancient gods alongside the saints of the Catholic church.

Dwelling Places of the Gods

The Lacandon Indians, who live today in the forests of Chiapas, in the far south of Mexico, are the last representatives of a Lowland Maya culture, dating from the Post-Classic era, which is at present facing extinction. During the colonial period their ancestors, who were originally from the Petén (the Guatemalan forest), could be found along the banks of the Río de la Pasión and the Usumacinta; they only moved into Chiapas in the late 18th century.

It is well known that the forests of Chiapas and the Petén are scattered

A ceramic model of the god Chac, from Mayapán.

A group of Lacandon Indians—five men and two women—photographed in 1882.

with ruined monuments (temples, pyramids, stelae), built by the ancient Maya during the Classic period (A.D. 250–900). The Lacandon Indians believe these structures to be the work of supernatural beings whom they call *k'uh* (gods). These gods once lived upon the earth, and their houses are still visible there today. The houses of the gods are the same as those of the "True Men" [the Indians themselves]; but instead of palm leaf roofs, the human eye can see only stone. It is not only the ruins that are worshiped by the Lacandon Indians. Equally sacred to them are great rocks that stand at the edge of a lake, caves used as tombs and ossuaries by the tribes who formerly occupied the Chiapas forest. The Lacandons say that the bones that lie strewn over the floor of the caves (for the tombs have been desecrated) are those of the gods, who pretended to die, though their spirits entered deep under the rock. As for the divinities who lived in Yaxchilán, they rose into the heavens. Men then began to communicate with the gods using pottery incense burners.

The expression "house of the gods" (*u y-atoch k'uh*) can describe either a temple (the hut where the incense burners are kept and where most religious rites are celebrated), or the ruins and caves where the spirits of the gods live, which were formerly the object of pilgrimages.

The ritual practices of the Lacandons are inspired by various pre-Cortésian religious traditions. After the decline of the Classic Maya civilization, in the 9th century A.D., the forest inhabitants who had survived the cataclysm (or who had recently arrived in the region) continued to visit the abandoned centers and perform simple rites there.…

As for the use of caves as a setting for rituals, as pilgrimage centers and sepulchres, "this dates back to the Middle Pre-Classic and continues to the end of the Late Classic (600 B.C.– A.D. 900)." To this very day the highland Indians of Chiapas and Guatemala hold the caves sacred.

I said that the expression "house of the gods" (*u y-atoch k'uh*) can refer either to the hut (temple) where the incense burners are stored, or to the rock or cave where the spirits of a family of gods are said to dwell. What is the connection between the incense burners and the holy caves? I will begin by describing the general appearance of the sacred caves that I visited in 1974 and 1979. It is certain that these were originally burial chambers, desecrated many times since then. At the entrance to the cave is a small mound of stones called *u mukulan* (the tomb), which is probably the source of the bones (skulls, jawbones, femurs) scattered all around. It is likely that offerings originally accompanied the remains of the body or bodies, but they have no doubt been stolen. Apart from a few fragments of pottery there is now no trace of these funerary gifts. On the other hand, the floor of the cave is littered with pottery and gourds, offered to the gods by the Lacandons, together with old abandoned incense burners.

At the back, against the rocky wall, stand the stone altars of the god and goddess, his wife, guardians of the cave and of the nearby lake. The stone erected to represent the god is taller than that symbolizing his wife. It is impossible to discern the original form of these statues, because they are completely covered with soot and the remains of burnt copal. The "True Men" burn incense on the *u-ho'or* (head) of the statue, inside a circle of small pebbles stuck onto the resinous substance. When they decide to make an incense burner for the god they have come to worship, they take some of these pebbles home with them and put them in the bottom of the clay pot, *u-*

lak-i k'uh (pot of the god) that will act as the new incense burner. It has a stylized anthropomorphic head, with a lower lip that juts out to receive the ritual offerings of food and drink. They can then communicate with the god, via the intermediary of the sacred stones, *u kanche'k'uh* (the seat of the god) contained within the incense burner, on which they burn the copal resin. During their rites the god's spirit descends and sits down on the stones (which is how these relics get their name).

We have supplied elsewhere a complete version of the mythology of the *Hach Winik*, such as it exists today. Their vision of the end of the world usually begins with an eclipse of the sun, which plunges the forest into total darkness. The men call upon their gods and burn copal in their incense burners, but all in vain, for they cannot prevent the jaguars of the heavens and of the Underworld from hunting them down and devouring them. Men and women who are still virgins are taken to Yaxchilán, where Hachakyum, the creator and supreme god, has them decapitated.

The gods paint their houses with their blood. Note that, during certain religious rites, the Lacandons paint their faces, tunics, incense burners and the pillars of their temples with anatta—an orange-red dye made from the fruits of a small tree, the *bixa orellana*. This is why they say: "The blood of men is the anatta of the gods." This myth depicts the gods as bloodthirsty beings who revel in the smell of human blood; and it evokes memories of the human sacrifices practiced by the Maya during the Post-Classic era. The souls of the men who are sacrificed at the end of the world are sent to the highest level of the cosmos, where it is always night.

The *Hach Winik* believe that the end of the present world is nigh. In the meantime several Lacandon families have converted to Christianity, believing that when the end of the world comes, their souls will go to heaven "with Jesus," instead of suffering the shadowy darkness, fear, and cold for all eternity.

Didier Boremanse
Les Vrais Hommes, 1986

Maya Prayers

The eminent British archaeologist and epigraphist J. Eric S. Thompson, to whom we owe many discoveries about the Maya calendar and script, was also very interested in the social and religious life of the Indians with whom he came into contact in the course of his research. He always insisted on the need to combine archaeology with the study of history and ethnography.

In the course of my stay at San Antonio and later when I had men from San Antonio as laborers in excavating at the site of Mountain Cow, I collected a number of prayers used in the yearly round of clearing the forest, burning the dry brush, and sowing. Typical are the prayers made before the forest is cut down to make the *milpa* [field] and addressed to the winds a month or more later when the felled brush is to be burned. Strong wind is essential, for if the dead brush does not burn well, it will be even harder to burn it a second time.

"O God, my father, my mother, Holy Huitz-Hok, lord of the hills and valleys, lord of the forest, be patient. I am doing as always has been done. Now I am making my offering [of copal] to you that you may know that I am aggravating your goodwill, but perhaps you will suffer it. I am about to damage you, I am about to work you so that I may live, but I pray that no wild animal of the forest follow my footsteps, that no snake perchance, nor scorpion perchance fall on me, nor perchance the axe nor perchance the machete cut me. With all my soul I am going to work you."

And "O God, holy wind, now I desire that you do your work for me. Where are you, you red wind, you white wind, you whirlwind? I do not know where you are—in the remotest end of the heavens, in the midst of the

Yucatecan Indian woman in ceremonial dress.

mighty hills, in the midst of the great valleys. Now I desire that you play with all your strength here where I have done my work."

In the first prayer the words "I am about to damage you" bring out the Maya's realization that in cutting down the forest he is doing harm to the surface of the earth, to the face of the earth god, Huitz-Hok, the mountain-valley god, the Mopan equivalent of Tzultacah. Another prayer refers to damaging the god's face. It has been affirmed that no primitive people has an appreciation of the beauty of nature, but I sometimes wonder how true that is. Here one might claim that the *milpa*-maker is merely apologizing for the physical damage he is about to do to the face of the earth god, but I think that beyond this he is apologizing for the scars he is inflicting on beauty, and that in converting a piece of forest with its trees, its lianas, and its bromelids, almost all of which have a name and a use, into a brown expanse of dead foliage and fallen tree trunks, he is well aware that he is destroying beauty....

Inquiry also brought out a large selection of myths and folktales, some of which were Maya, but others European and quite a few of the Br'er Rabbit type which were probably brought to Central America by African slaves. One of the most interesting cycles of legends recounted the life and adventures of the sun god when he dwelled on earth before there was any sun in the sky. As a young man he courted the girl who later became the moon, and persuaded her to flee with him (he changed into a hummingbird which the girl took to her room when it was wounded by a pellet from her father's blowgun). After various adventures they settled down to married life, but the moon goddess was a fickle wanton. She had an affair with her brother-in-law, the god of the planet Venus, and later eloped with the king vulture.

Metaphors

Maya is a pleasant language with some charming metaphors. A girl or a boy approaching marriage age is called "maize plant coming into flower"; a meddler is rebuked with the words, "Why are you wearing a loincloth that is not yours?"; a red-hot ember is called a fire flower. Infinity is more than the hairs on a deer; a man will speak of his father's being dead as "my father's bones are piled up." A clever business-man is said to have a snout that sticks out (cf. our expression "a good nose for business"); and in that connection it is interesting that the Maya god of merchants has a sort of nose like Pinocchio's, and one of the names of the chief Aztec god of merchants was "he with the pointed nose." Old men are called mighty rocks; a hard-hearted person is "he with a tree-trunk face"; when a person forgets what he is going to say he remarks that the bat carried off his story.

With a careful choice of words one can reduce ill effects. If a tiger-ant bites you, say, "A dry leaf bit me," for if you admit it was the bite of a tiger-ant, you will feel it for several days. A similar psychological routing of the odor of skunk is achieved by ignoring the skunk and remarking instead, "How sweet is the scent of the squash seed my grandmother is toasting," a sentence which sounds as though it came out of French for Beginners or the Sayings of

Confucius. Strange, too, that we discard the seed of squash and marrow, but the Maya consider them extraordinarily tasty. The Maya understand the pangs of love, for the word *yail* means both love and pain.

Sometimes a knowledge of such terms helps in the interpretation of Maya art symbols. For instance, axe blades in Maya sculpture sometimes terminate in maizelike vegetation. The explanation of this probably lies in the fact that the word *tzuc* means the beard of an ear of maize, a horse's mane, as well as the back of an axe blade.

The present-day Maya retain some of the gestures of their ancestors. I noticed in the village of Socotz that when the children entered a hut to say good morning or, at the hour of the angelus, to say good evening to their parents or other adults, they stood feet together with arms folded across their breasts and tips of fingers under forearms. Exactly similar poses occur in ancient Maya sculpture and on painted vessels, and always, I believe, are those of persons apparently of humble rank. So there in Socotz, almost in the shadow of the old Maya center of Benque Viejo, that ancient pose was still used in the ceremonial greeting of morning and at the moment of sunset....

Continuity with the past was what confronted me the deeper I penetrated the Maya pattern of life. Continuity with a subtle inflection. When those children of Socotz stood with folded arms, the thatch above their heads was no different from that of Maya huts of a millennium ago—both had that purple-gray tone of weathered cabbage palm, but the angelus bell had rung in the village, and by the road a soft-drink stand reared its monstrous frame of rusted sheets of corrugated iron.

J. Eric S. Thompson
Maya Archaeologist, 1963

Death of a Maya

Tzotzil, by Juan Perez Jolote, describes the traditions of a people whose culture is undergoing change under the influence of our own civilization. The Chamula are a group of over 16,000 Indians who speak the Tzotzil language and live in parajes *(territorial divisions of the Indian villages in the center of Chiapas state), scattered over the slopes of the high plateaus of San*

A Tzotzil Indian.

Cristobal, near Ciudad las Casas. The village of Chamula is the center of this community. The following account was recorded in 1952, but it describes events that took place between 1910 and 1920.

The land of my ancestors lies near the *Gran Pueblo* (Chamula) in the sector of Cuchulmtic. The house where I was born has not changed. When my father died we divided up what he had left; my brothers took the roof beams and walls that belonged to them, but I rebuilt the house in the same place with a new straw roof and walls of dried mud. Sheep were allowed to graze all over the garden, to manure the soil.... Everything is exactly as I remember it when I was a child; nothing has changed. When I die and my soul returns, it will find the paths I used and recognize my house.

After the Death of My Father

In the yard outside the house some of the women were grinding maize, while others killed chickens to feed the people who had come for the burial; my mother was mending my father's clothes and the *chamarros* [rectangular woolen cloth with a slit in the middle for the head, woven on looms dating from before the Conquest], and putting his things in order for the journey. [The Chamula believe that the dead must walk a long way and cross a dog-infested lake; to get from one bank to the other they must climb onto the back of one of the dogs.]

A table was set up next to him, so he could eat; chicken was put on one plate, tortillas in another, with salt in a saucer. After my father had been served, we ate.

The sun was setting; so we set out. When men die old, their souls get tired on the journey, so they must be given plenty to drink. My aunt, Maria Perez Jolote, gave water to my father each time we stopped for a rest. They would lift the lid of the coffin, and she would sprinkle his mouth with water three times, using a laurel leaf that she dipped into a *huacal* [gourd].

When we got close to the cemetery, my uncle Marcos took the string bag in which I had put the provisions; he removed the small basket that held the *huacal and* took from it the cooked dishes, which he began to count; there were twelve portions of tortilla and three of *pozol* [drink made of maize]. He lifted the lid of the coffin and my father's *chamarro*, and beneath them, on his right side, he put the dishes with the *pozol* and the tortillas. Then he said: "This is to pay for your *chicha* [drink based on sugar cane], your lemons, your bananas, and your food; this is so you can buy anything you need."

We arrived at the great cross in the cemetery and we set down the coffin. Then a candle was lit, and all the women wept around the coffin while the men helped to dig the grave. Only a few more moments, and the Chultotic [sun] would enter the Olontic [kingdom of the dead]; the dead cannot be buried before it has entered there, or their souls will remain on the earth. My aunt arranged the *chamarros* in the coffin; all the clothes my father had worn were to go with him.

The sun had set. There were red clouds in the sky. When they had gone dark, we lowered the coffin and began to throw the earth back over it. The women ceased all their cries and lamentations, so that the soul would not return. When the grave was full we firmed the earth down well, then washed our hands. By the time we returned home, it was night.

Juan Perez Jolote,
Tzotzil (tales from the life of a
Mexican Indian,
recorded by Ricardo Pozas), 1952

Tzotzil Indians meeting in a village in Chiapas.

Further Reading

Bernal, Ignacio, *A History of Mexican Archaeology: The Vanished Civilizations of Middle America*, Thames and Hudson, New York, 1983

Brunhouse, Robert, *In Search of the Maya*, Ballantine, New York, 1976

Coe, Michael D., *Lords of the Underworld: Masterpieces of Classic Mayan Ceramics*, Princeton University Press, New Jersey, 1978

———, *The Maya*, Thames and Hudson, Ltd, London, 1987

Fash, William L., *Scribes, Warriors and Kings: The City of Copan and the Ancient Maya*, Thames and Hudson, Ltd, London, 1991

Hammond, Norman, *Ancient Maya Civilization*, Rutgers University Press, New Brunswick, New Jersey, 1982

Houston, Stephen D., *Maya Glyphs*, University of California Press, Berkeley, 1989

Ivanoff, Pierre, *Mayan Enigma: The Search for a Lost Civilization*, Delacorte, New York, 1971

———, *Monuments of Civilization: Maya*, Grosset and Dunlap, New York, 1973

Jones, Christopher, *Deciphering Maya Hieroglyphs*, University Museum of the University of Pennsylvania, 1984

Miller, Mary E., *The Art of Mesoamerica, From Olmec to Aztec*, Thames and Hudson, New York, 1986

———, *The Murals of Bonampak*, Thames and Hudson, New York, 1986

Morley, Sylvanus G., and George W. Brainerd, *The Ancient Maya*, Stanford University Press, California, 1983

Morris, William F., Jr., *Living Maya*, Harry N. Abrams, New York, 1987

Proskouriakoff, Tatiana, *An Album of Maya Architecture*, University of Oklahoma Press, Norman, Oklahoma, 1976

———, *A Study of Classic Maya Sculpture*, repr. of 1950 ed., AMS Press, New York

Schele, Linda, and David A. Freidel, *A Forest of Kings: The Untold Story of the Maya*, Morrow, New York, 1990

Schele, Linda, and Mary E. Miller, *The Blood of Kings: Dynasty and Ritual in Maya Art*, Kimbell Art Museum, Fort Worth, Texas, 1986

Spinden, Herbert J., *A Study of Maya Art: Its Subject Matter and Historical Development*, Dover, New York, 1975

Stuart, George C., and Gene S. Stuart, *The Mysterious Maya*, National Geographic Society, Washington, D. C., 1977

List of Illustrations

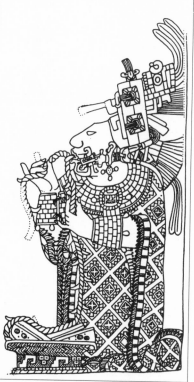

Index

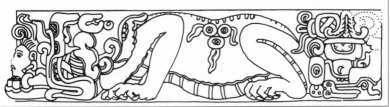

Acknowledgments

We would like to thank the following for their assistance in producing this book: Marie-France Fauvet Berthelot, curator of the Musée de l'Homme, Paris; the staff of the Bibliothèque du Musée de l'Homme; Alfred Fierro, curator of the Société de Géographie, Paris; Jean-Claude Lemagny, curator of the Cabinet des Estampes, Bibliothèque Nationale, Paris; Linda Schele, professor of art history at the University of Austin, Texas; Merle Greene Robertson, director of the Precolumbian Art Research Institute, San Francisco; Linda Schele and Mary E. Miller, *The Blood of Kings*, Kimbell Art Museum, Fort Worth, 1986; *Popol Vuh*, transl. © 1985 by Dennis Tedlock, reprinted by permission of Simon and Schuster, Inc., New York, 1985; J. E. S. Thompson, *Maya Archaeologist*, Robert Hale (Publishers), London, and University of Oklahoma Press, Norman, 1963

Photograph Credits

Claude Baudez, eminent archaeologist and head of research at France's Centre National de la Recherche Scientifique, has studied the remains of the little-known civilizations of Mesoamerica in Costa Rica and Honduras. Since 1971 he has devoted himself entirely to research into the Maya. He was codirector of the excavations carried out on the site of Toniná (Mexico), and was in charge of the program to explore and restore Copán (Honduras). He is coauthor, with P. Becquelin, of *Les Mayas*, 1984.

Sydney Picasso was the official photographer of the Franco-Brazilian archaeological mission to Lagoa Santa. Between 1974 and 1980 she was a research assistant at the Ecole des Hautes Etudes en Sciences Sociales, and since then she has been working for the Centre National de la Recherche Scientifique on a program on the rock art of South America.

For Bazile and Xavier

Translated from the French by Caroline Palmer

Project Manager: Sharon AvRutick
Typographic Designer: Elissa Ichiyasu
Design Assistant: Tricia McGillis
Editorial Assistant: Jennifer Stockman

Library of Congress Catalog Card Number: 91–75505
ISBN 0–8109–2841–8

Published in 1992 by Harry N. Abrams, Incorporated, New York
A Times Mirror Company

Printed and bound in Italy by Editoriale Libraria, Trieste

"We commenced work [in Quiriguá] early in February, which is considered to be the beginning of the dry season."

erected these elaborate monuments? The auth...
explorers to investigate; and artists, poets, an...
travelers were quick to follow. In the 19th cer...
adventurers had the singleminded dedication...
Their passion was to benefit science.

English archaeologist Alfred Perceval Maud...
Palenque, Copán, Chichén Itzá, and Quirigu...
cleared the undergrowth, took photographs, ...
and took notes, all with extraordinary precisi...
de Monjas [in Chichén Itzá] made us an exce...
house," he wrote, "and…we were even able to...
ourselves quite comfortable."